Emily

DISCARD

MS GULF COAST COMMUNITY COLLEGE
JEFFERSON DAVIS CAMPUS LIBRARY

Mysticism in Blake and Wordsworth

JACOMINA KORTELING

HASKELL HOUSE
Publishers of Scholarly Books
NEW YORK
1966

published by
HASKELL HOUSE
Publishers of Scholarly Books
30 East 10th Street • New York, N. Y. 10003

PRINTED IN UNITED STATES OF AMERICA

CONTENTS

CHAP.		PAGE
I.	GENERAL INTRODUCTION	1
II.	INTRODUCTION TO BLAKE'S WORKS	7
III.	WILLIAM BLAKE. SONGS OF INNOCENCE	15
IV.	SONGS OF EXPERIENCE	24
V.	SOME EARLY PROPHETIC BOOKS	35
VI.	THE FALL	43
VII.	THE FOUR ZOAS. THE EMANATIONS	49
VIII.	THE REDEMPTION	53
IX.	NATURE	79
X.	HIS VISIONS	88
XI.	WILLIAM WORDSWORTH. NATURE	100
XII.	THE CHILD	130
XIII.	MAN	144
XIV.	CONCLUSION	154
	BIBLIOGRAPHY	170

First Published 1928

HASKELL HOUSE PUBLISHERS LTD.
Publishers of Scarce Scholarly Books
280 LAFAYETTE STREET
NEW YORK, N. Y. 10012

Library of Congress Catalog Card Number: **68-2111**

Standard Book Number 8383-0577-6

Printed in the United States of America

Chapter I

GENERAL INTRODUCTION

Caroline Spurgeon says in *Mysticism in English Literature*: "Among English writers and poets the only two who fulfil the strict definition of a mystic are Wordsworth and Blake."[1] This saying suggested to me the present study.

Before entering upon my subject proper it will be necessary to state what is meant by mysticism. The word is so wide in its meaning, so exhaustless in its associations, that often it has lost clear and definite outline. Not seldom is it tinged with a shade of contempt, as implying exalted, abnormal psychic condition, creating morbid phantasies, which satisfy the mystic's feverish craving after spiritual excitement. Sometimes its meaning is lowered to the materialistic level of table-rapping and ghostly vision. Often it is not realised that it comprises the deepest consciousness of man, his highest aspirations, his most luminous revelations, that the mystic experience is life in its essence, life in the embrace of the supersensuous world, in which it has its being.

The word draws its origin from Greece. In the Greek mysteries a mystic was an initiate in the secrets of divine things. The Neoplatonists took over the word and through them it passed into Christian terminology, retaining its essential meaning.

Many writers on the subject have tried to circumscribe the rich and varied life which mysticism suggests. Inge says: "Mysticism has its origin in that which is the raw material of all religion, and perhaps of all philosophy and art as well, namely that dim consciousness of the beyond, which is part of our nature as human beings."[2] "Religious mysticism may be defined as

[1] Caroline F. E. Spurgeon, *Mysticism in English Literature*, p. 11. (See p. 102).
[2] W. R. Inge, *Christian Mysticism*, p. 5.

the attempt to realise the presence of the living God in the soul and in nature, or, more generally, as the attempt to realise, in thought and feeling, the immanence of the temporal in the eternal, and of the eternal in the temporal." [1] Eternal Life in the midst of Time is the secret of Christianity," [2] says Harnack, by which he means Christianity as it is mystically experienced, in which words he unveils the secret of all mystical life. Lasson defines it as an "aspiration to see the Absolute by pure spiritual apprehension," [3] Professor de Graaf says about it: „De mystiek is een bezinning op het allerinnerlijkste, een terugkeer tot die bronnen van het godsdienstig leven, waaruit elke vernieuwing weer komen moet," and Evelyn Underhill understands it to be "the expression of the innate tendency of the human spirit towards complete harmony with the transcendental order, whatever be the theological formula under which that order is understood. This tendency, in great mystics, gradually captures the whole field of consciousness; it dominates their life, and, in the experience called 'mystic union' attains its end. Whether that end be called the God of Christianity, the World-soul of Pantheism, the Absolute of Philosophy, the desire to attain it and the movement towards it — so long as this is a genuine life process and not an intellectual speculation — is the proper subject of mysticism. I believe this movement to represent the true line of development of the highest form of human consciousness." [5]

We see that all these definitions are identical in their ultimate acceptation of mysticism as being an inner intuitive knowledge of transcendental life, that soul's experience through which man is lifted from the world of appearances into the eternal realms of spiritual vision.

To different mystics the ineffable revelation has come in different ways, because, as Evelyn Underhill says, "the angles at which consciousness is set towards Reality are infinite and

---

[1] Inge, *Christian Mysticism*, p. 5.
[2] Harnack, *Das Wesen des Christentums*, p. 5, quoted by Evelyn Underhill in *The Mystic Way*, p. 33.
[3] Inge, *Christian Mysticism*, p. 342.
[4] H. T. De Graaf, *Levensrichting*, p. 8.
[5] Evelyn Underhill, *Mysticism*, Preface, p. X.

every teacher gives us the system which he represents, not as a demonstration of scientific truth, but as an artist, through a temperament." [1] Yet in the inexhaustibility of personality, in the variety of spiritual apprehension, there is a central unity where differences meet, because they contain an aspect of the truth, which is changeless and timeless. The meeting-point of all mystics is a common revealed knowledge of a spiritual unity underlying diversity of appearances and consequently of man's partaking in the nature of the Divine. The mystic feels himself like that one ripple on the boundless deep, that

> "Feels that the deep is boundless, and itself
> For ever changing form, but evermore
> One with the boundless motion of the deep." [2]

Besides, all of them enjoy the capacity of loving in a superior degree, because "the true hyrophant of the mysteries of God is love," [3] love, the sun which illuminates what was dark, reveals what was hidden and gives life to what was dead, the one grand, all-embracing, life-giving force, in which is reflected the ground of being, in which and through which man beholds the ineffable light. [4] But mostly the gates of Heaven are not opened to the mystic, as soon as this powerful love begins to surge within him. Love, the touch of the Eternal, creates a craving after that which is its being and from the moment the mystic has been seized by the spirit, he does not rest, before, often after laborious ascent, he has reached the mountain-top, where the Heart of his desire lures him on, till he is hidden in the mystery of His love, united with Him in perfect union.

Different stages can be marked on the upward way. Evelyn Underhill makes a division of five, which I shall state in brief: 1) the awakening to a divine reality; 2) the consequent purgation of the Self, when it realizes its own imperfections; 3) an enhanced return of the sense of the divine order, after the Self has achieved

---

[1] Evelyn Underhill, *The Mystic Way*, p. 1.
[2] Alfred Tennyson, *The ancient Sage*.
[3] Inge, *Christian Mysticism*, p. 3.
[4] See *the first Epistle of St. John* IV, 7, 8.

its detachment from the world; 4) the "Dark Night of the Soul," or the crucifixion of the Self in the absence of the divine; 5) the complete union with Truth, the attainment of that which the third state had perceived as a possibilty.[1] Foster Damon, the latest exponent of Blake's philosophy and symbolism applies this division to the development of the poet's mystic consciousness.

The mysticism that is comprised within the scope of this scheme is especially that kind which is mostly attached to the great devotional mystics, those who live the mystic life in its complete fulfilment, who are absolutely immersed in it and whose subtle spiritualism blossomed forth in such wondrous bloom in the Middle-Ages for instance. They were pre-eminently religious temperaments, and the subtlety, deepness and tender sweetness of their religious feeling made them poets whose devout songs are among the brightest jewels of ghostly lyricism.

But there is another kind of mystics. It will be clearly seen from the afore-mentioned observations that the poets, the artists in general, will partake more or less of the nature of mystics. They, the singers of beauty, whether it is the beauty of the visible world or the beauty that shines in the tears and sings in the laughter of all that lives, will often grasp something of the hidden meaning which underlies the splendour and gloom, the rejoicing and sobbing of the miracle which is life, will catch a glimpse, in flashes of inspiration, of the Abiding in the sweeping rush of Time. Their keen susceptibility to impressions of beauty, their emotional profundity and vital imaginative power bring them to the depth, where the poet and mystic meet and break into rapt song of pious adoration. Listen how Emily Brontë, the recluse of the lonely moors, one of England's deepest mystic poets, sings of the supreme experience that comes to her in the spirit-laden atmosphere of even-tide.

---

[1] Evelyn Underhill, *Mysticism*, p. 205.
S. Foster Damon, *William Blake: his Philosophy and Symbols*, p. 2.
[2] Evelyn Underhill abandons "the time-honoured, three-fold division of the mystic way" "which were codified by the Neoplatonists and after them by the mediaeval mystics, as Purgation, Illumination and Ecstasy." (Evelyn Underhill, *Mysticism*, p. 112.)

"He comes with western winds, with evening's wandering airs,
With that clear dusk of heaven that brings the thickest stars.
Winds take a pensive tone, and stars a tender fire,
And visions rise, and change, that kill me with desire.
. . . .
But, first, a hush of peace — a soundless calm descends;
The struggle of distress, and fierce impatience ends;
Mute music soothes my breast — unuttered harmony,
That I could never dream, till Earth was lost to me.

Then dawns the Invisible; the Unseen its truth reveals;
My outward sense is gone, my inward essence feels:
Its wings are almost free — its home, its harbour found,
Measuring the gulf, it stoops and dares the final bound.

Oh! dreadful is the check — intense the agony —
When the ear begins to hear, and the eye begins to see;
When the pulse begins to throb, the brain to think again;
The soul to feel the flesh, and the flesh to feel the chain."[1]

According to the different ways by which Reality is approached, mystics have been divided into philosophical mystics, beauty- and love-mystics, nature-mystics, devotional and religious mystics.[2] Division will have this advantage that it gives an easy survey of the wide field that mysticism covers, but we must never forget that the living moveableness of an inner experience can never be entirely confined in fixed classifications, that often different classes overlap each other, that in each life works its mysterious, endless variety of impressions and emotions. Caroline Spurgeon classes Emily Brontë among the *philosophical* mystics, those who express their thoughts and feelings, to a certain extent, not predominantly, in philosophical language, which appeals both to the intellect and to the feeling.

A place amongst them is also given to Tennyson, who testifies, perhaps less subtilely than Emile Brontë, but with not less fervent devotion to his dearest and nearest Possession in that fine poem, *the Higher Pantheism*:

"Speak to Him thou for He hears, and Spirit with Spirit can meet —
Closer is He than breathing, and nearer than hands and feet.

[1] Emily Brontë, *The Prisoner*, quoted by Caroline Spurgeon in *Mysticism in English Literature*, pp. 82, 83.
[2] Caroline Spurgeon, *Mysticism in English Literature*, p. 33.

And the ear of man cannot hear, and the eye of man cannot see;
But if we could see and hear, this Vision — were it not He?".[1]

Rossetti was often moved into the mystic experience by the *beauty* in a woman's face. Keats deified beauty in the famous lines from the *Ode on a Grecian Urn*:

"Beauty is truth, truth Beauty, that is all
Ye know on earth, and all ye need to know."

Coventry Patmore saw in *love* between man and woman the symbol of the higher love between man and God. Wordsworth is the greatest *nature*-mystic of England, he who found in the "visions of the hills," and "souls of lonely places" the ground of his being, the essence of life. Blake is ranked by Caroline Spurgeon among the *religious* mystics.[2] It is difficult to place him, who is so entirely different from the others. Certainly he is a religious mystic, as he avails himself to a great extent of Christian terminology, and believes in Christ as the inner Saviour of his soul and of the soul of the world. But his doctrines sometimes sound so heretical, his mentality is often so different from what we are used to find in religious mystics, that we cannot class him under this heading without drawing attention to the fact of this deviation from the beaten path. Often it is not easy to follow him in the many intricate windings of his obscure course, several lose patience and return before they have reached the Light it leads to, but those who take into their hands the end of the golden string which the poet gives to all those who wish for it and wind it into a ball, will be lead by its shining light up to the gate of Heaven.

"I give you the end of a golden string:
Only wind it into a ball,
It will lead you in at Heaven's gate,
Built in Jerusalem's wall."[3]

---

[1] Quoted by Caroline Spurgeon in *Mysticism in English Literature*, p. 88.
[2] *Ibid.*, p. 129.
[3] *Jerusalem, To the Christians*, introduction to chapter 4.

Chapter II

INTRODUCTION TO BLAKE'S WORKS

The figure of William Blake, the painter-poet-mystic, notwithstanding the great appreciation he enjoys in recent criticism, is still shrouded in mystery for many readers. To Wordsworth was given during his life-time already the place among England's poets which was his due, with Blake it was different, therefore it seems desirable to say a few words about him by way of introduction.

To the majority of readers, and even to professional readers, men of letters, Blake is often no more than a name, associated with vague notions of a wild visionary, living in an obscure spirit-world, a man whose poetical productions may be safely ignored as the morbid phantasies of a feverish mind. Many do not realise that, notwithstanding his serious defects, he was one of the great mystic poets of his time, that with the piercing glance of the prophet he looked into the hidden promise of the age to come, that in the mystic's illumination he beheld the inner fact of the universe. His time ignored him, to a great extent at least, and after his death there was a period of almost absolute silence respecting him, till the publication of Alexander Gilchrist's *The Life of William Blake* in 1863 showed that not all interest in him was dead. This suggestive biography was the stimulant to an enthusiastic Blake-cult, which meant a gradual unveiling of the truth of his art, often hidden beneath an obscure covering, and a subsequent recognition of him by many as one of England's great poets and mystics. [1]

---

[1] Evelyn Underhill, Charles Gardner, Caroline Spurgeon, Foster Damon, for instance, rank him very high as a mystic, Inge does not mention him, and Helen White among others denies him a prominent place in the mystical field. Here follow the principal books and essays written on Blake after Gilchrist's biography:
A. C. Swinburne, *William Blake, a critical Essay*. London, Camden Hot-

8   INTRODUCTION TO BLAKE'S WORKS

The obscurity of William Blake's poetry may be traced to different sources: after the apathy and intellectualism of the eighteenth century he was the first to take up again the flaming torch of mysticism, which after the so-called methaphysical poets in

ten, Picadilly, 1868, second edition, London, Chatto and Windus, 1906.
E. J. Ellis and W. B. Yeats, *The Works of William Blake, poetic, symbolic, and critical*. London, Quaritch, 1893. This book is very important as being the first to give an explanation of Blake's symbolic system.
A. Story, *William Blake, his Life, Character and Genius*. London, Swan, Sonnenschein and Co., 1893.
Richard Garnett, *William Blake, Painter and Poet*. London, Seeley and Co., New-York, Macmillan and Co. 1895, the Portfolio Monographs, no. 22.
Rudolf Kassner, *Die Mystik, die Künstler und das Leben, über Englische Dichter und Maler im 19 Jahrhundert*. Leipzig, Diederichs, 1900.
Helene Richter, *William Blake*. Strassburg, Heitz und Mündel, 1906.
Stefan Zweig, *Die Visionaire Kunst Philosophie William Blakes*. Leipzig, Julius Zeitler, 1906.
P. Berger, *William Blake, Mysticisme et Poésie*. Paris, société française d'imprimerie et de librairie, 1907.
Stopford Brooke, *Studies in Poetry*. London, Duckworth and Company, 1907.
Arthur Symons, *William Blake*. London, Constable and Company Ltd., New-York, Dutton and Company, 1907.
Greville Mac Donald, *The Sanity of William Blake*. London, A. C. Tifield, 1908.
Evelyn Underhill, *Mysticism. A Study in the Nature and Development of Man's spiritual Conciousness*. London, Methuen and Co., 1911.
Publications of the Blake-society, Olney, Thomas Wright, the first meeting of which was held on the 12th of August, 1912.
Lafcadio Hearn, *Interpretations of Literature*, selected and edited with an introduction by John Erskine. London, William Heineman, 1916. Essay vol. 1. *Blake, the first English Mystic*.
Charles Gardner, *Vision and Vesture, a Study of William Blake in Modern Thought*. London, J. M. Dent and Sons, 1917.
Charles Gardner, *William Blake, the Man*. London, Dent and Sons, New-York, Dutton and Co., 1919.
Geoffrey Keynes, *Bibliography of Blake*. Grolier Club of New York, 1921.
Caroline F. E. Spurgeon, *Mysticism in English Literature*. Cambridge, University Press, 1922.
S. Foster Damon, *William Blake: his Philosophy and Symbols*. London, Bombay, Sidney, Constable and Co., 1924.
Osbert Burdett, *William Blake*. London, Macmillan and Co., 1926.
Mona Wilson, *The Life of William Blake*. Nonesuch Press, 1927.
Helen C. White, *The Mysticism of William Blake*, Madison, University of Wisconsin Studies, 1927.

the seventeenth century, such as Donne, Crashaw, Vaughan, and their contemporaries, the Cambridge Platonists, representatives of whom are John Smith, Benjamin Whichcote and Henry More, seemed to have been extinguished. It is true, with the dawn of romanticism, the new spirit with its aspirations after the infinite, its yearnings after the ideal, the mystic note was again heard here and there, as for instance in Cowper's poetry, but Blake's songs were the first in which it was rung with all the grandeur, the flaming ardour of the religious enthusiast, for whom the mystic feeling is the predominating heart's emotion, the life of his very soul, the one reality. In this he outsoared the spirit of his time and his time proved to be unable to appreciate him. Besides, the symbolism in which he tried to express his extraordinary imaginative conceptions is often obscure to such a degree as to be but partially understood. But in connection with this we must not overlook the fact that we do not know in how far Blake has explained his symbolism in the bulk of his whole work, as probably we do not possess it in its entirety. To Crabb Robinson he spoke of seven epics as long as Homer's and of twenty tragedies as long as Macbeth [1] which he had written, but which have not come down to us, and which may have been destroyed by his friend Tatham, to whom after his death his wife gave most of her husband's remaining manuscripts and paintings, and who was shocked at their heretical blasphemies and moral defectiveness. Another factor which contributed towards Blake's obscurity is the fact that his books were not published in the ordinary way. When he was in great uneasiness of mind as to how to bring his works before the public, deliverance came to him in a characteristically Blakean way in the form of his beloved dead brother Robert, who appeared to him in the spirit with a message which solved the problem that had been harassing him during so many days and nights. Henceforth he was to be his own printer and publisher. As unique as was his work was the method of giving it shape. Not the mechanic printer's hand was to visualize the rich dreams of his fervid mind, the poet and painter himself was to create the form in which they were to

[1] Crabb Robinson, *Reminiscences*, quoted by Gilchrist in *The Life of William Blake*, p. 368.

appear. His method of revealing his genius to the world "consisted in a species of engraving in relief both words and designs. The verse was written and the designs and marginal embellishments outlined on the copper with an impervious liquid, probably the ordinary stopping-out varnish of engravers. Then all the white parts or lights, the remainder of the plate that is, were eaten away with aquafortis or other acid, so that the outline of letter and design was left prominent, as in stereotype. From these plates he printed off in any tint, yellow, brown, blue, required to be the prevailing, or ground-colour in his facsimiles; red he used for the letter-press. The page was then coloured up by hand in imitation of the original drawing, with more or less variety of detail in the local hues." [1]

In this way those unique books came into being, each part of which is aflame with the poet's genius, where the design breaks into song and the song is visualized in the "eyemusic" of the design. A very limited number of copies were made in this way, so that his works were only accessible to few readers in his time. The difficulty of getting access to his works continued in after times, though in a less degree. Only the year 1925 saw for the first time a complete and accurate edition of Blake's works in print. [2]

[1] Gilchrist, *The Life of William Blake*, p. 71.
[2] Geoffrey Keynes, *The Writings of William Blake*. London, Nonesuch Press, 1925.
Here follow the principal editions:
Dr. Garth Wilkinson, *Songs of Innocence and Experience*. London, 1839.
Gilchrist, *Blake's shorter Poems*, 1863. (part of *The Life of William Blake*)
The Aldine edition, *Blake's shorter Poems*. London, Bell and sons, 1874.
E. J. Ellis and W. B. Yeats, *The Works of William Blake, poetic, symbolic and critical*. London, Quaritch, 1893.
It is important as being the first edition which contains the 'Prophetic Books.'
A. G. B. Russell and E. R. D. Maclagan, *Jerusalem*. London, Bullen, 1904.
John Sampson, *The Poetical Works of William Blake*. Oxford, Clarendon Press, 1905.
This is a very good edition, but Sampson gives only extracts from the *Prophetic Books*.
John Sampson, *The lyrical Poems of William Blake*, with an introduction by Walter Raleigh. Oxford, University Press, 1905.
Edwin J. Ellis, *The poetical Works of William Blake*. London, Chatto and Windus, 1906.

All the above-mentioned things may have been elements in the cause of his obscurity, but they do not explain all. What remains is the mystery of personality. If we think that Blake was not understood by any of his contemporaries, we are mistaken. Many of the influential men of the time appreciated him, saw in his work flashes of extraordinary genius. Among others Romney, Fuseli, Flaxman and Lawrence were admirers of his art, Wordsworth, Crabb Robinson, Lamb and Coleridge felt the power of his poetry. On the whole he was better known as a painter, an engraver, than as a poet. But the admiration of many of the able men of his time could not secure for him a place among them. His greatness was destined to remain enclosed within the convent-walls which after all the seclusion of his spirit erected round it. Though he asserted to the very boundary of normality the power of his own art, placing himself on a level with the great geniuses of the world, yet he did not push his way into that world, which, besides genius, requires something else of an artist, if he is to obtain to fame. It was to a certain extent in consequence of the strong faith with which he remained faithful to his most sacred convictions that Blake was denied during his lifetime the place that was his due. His contemporary, Allan Cunningham, says of him: "The eminence which it had been the first ambition of his youth to climb, was visible before him, and he saw on its ascent or on its summit those who had started earlier in the race of fame. He felt conscious of his own merit, but was not aware of the thousand obstacles which were ready to inter-

---

A. G. B. Russell, *The Letters of William Blake, together with a life by Frederick Tatham*. London, Methuen, 1906.
A. G. B. Russell and E. R. D. Maclagan, *Milton*. London, Bullen, 1907.
D. J. Sloss and J. P. R. Wallis, *The prophetic Writings of William Blake* in two volumes, edited with a general introduction, glossarial index of symbols, commentary and appendices. Oxford, Clarendon Press, 1926.
Geoffrey Keynes, *Letters from William Blake to Thomas Butts, 1800—1803*, printed in Facsimile with an Introductory Note by Geoffrey Keynes. Oxford, Clarendon Press, 1927.
Keynes, *Blake's complete Poetry and Prose in one Volume*. London, Nonesuch Press, 1927.
I have used Sampson's edition for the shorter poems, Sloss and Wallis's for the prophetic writings.

pose. He thought that he had but to sing songs and draw designs, and become great and famous. The crosses which genius is heir to had been wholly unforeseen, and they befell him early; he wanted the skill of hand and fine tact of fancy and taste, to impress upon the offspring of his thoughts that popular shape which gives such productions immediate circulation."[1] Foster Damon thinks it "a curious puzzle to explain why Blake was not better known in his own day. He seems to have come into contact with many of the famous and influential, he always won some recognition of his genius from them, and he was always forgotten almost at once."[2] And afterwards, having mentioned the names of several enthusiastic admirers: "What became of the enthusiasm of all these people? Blake made no effort to utilize it. And they in their turn usually looked upon the fascination of this or that work of Blake's as merely a curiosity which happened to be personally appealing. And so Blake was passed by as something extraordinary; but eccentric, and not of ultimate importance."[3]

We may be inclined to think that with his eccentricity he stood in his own way, but the very moment our thought tends towards that direction, we feel the greatness which lurked in his absolute ignoring of the world's favour. His character was one that could not make allowances for deviation from the path which he saw as the right one. Any tampering with the world meant loss of spiritual power. And he had the courage to remain true to himself. Blake was a bad critic. He did not see his own shortcomings, and he often failed to recognize another's greatness, but yet, the thoroughness with which he clung to his deepest convictions is admirable, and his very indomitable individualism is one of the things which make up the fascination of his unique personality.

"What is the Divine Spirit? is the Holy Ghost any other than an Intellectual Fountain? What is the Harvest of the Gospel

---

[1] Allan Cunningham, *The Life of William Blake* from *Lives of the most eminent British Painters, Sculptors and Architects*, quoted by Symons, *William Blake*, p. 401.
[2] Foster Damon, *William Blake, etc.*, p. 242.
[3] *Ibid.*, p. 243.

and its Labours? What is that Talent which it is a curse to hide? What are the Treasures of Heaven which we are to lay up for ourselves? are they any other than Mental Studies and Performances? What are all the Gifts of the Gospel? Are they not all Mental Gifts? Is God a Spirit who must be worshipped in Spirit and in Truth, and are not the Gifts of the Spirit Everything to Man? O ye Religious, discountenance every one among you who shall pretend to despise Art and Science! I call upon you in the Name of Jesus! What is the Life of Man but Art and Science? is it Meat and Drink? is not the Body more than Raiment? What is Mortality but the things relating to the Body which Dies? What is Immortality but the things relating to the Spirit which Lives Eternally? What is the Joy of Heaven but Improvement in the things of the Spirit? What are the Pains of Hell but Ignorance, Bodily Lust, Idleness, and devastation of the things of the Spirit?"

He did not shirk the spiritual duty which he felt incumbent upon him of leaving his patron Hayley, who helped him financially, but who intercepted the light of his vision. That it required courage is revealed in a letter he wrote from Felpham to his friend Mr. Butts. This letter reveals too that he was firmly determined to act up to the promptings of his deepest convictions. I quote part of it: "That I cannot live without doing my duty to lay up treasures in heaven, is certain and determined, and to this I have long made up my mind. And why this should be made an objection to me, while drunkenness, lewdness, gluttony, and even idleness itself, does not hurt other men, let Satan himself explain. The thing I have most at heart — more than life, or all that seems to make life comfortable without — is the interest of true religion and science. And whenever anything appears to affect that interest (especially if I myself omit any duty to my station as a soldier of Christ), it gives me the greatest of torments. I am not ashamed, afraid, or averse to tell you what ought to be told — that I am under the direction of messengers from heaven, daily and nightly. But the nature of such things is not, as some suppose, without trouble or care. Temptations are on the

---

[1] *Jerusalem, To the Christians.*

right hand and on the left. Behind, the sea of time and space roars and follows swiftly. He who keeps not right onwards is lost; and if our footsteps slide in clay, how can we do otherwise than fear and tremble?.... If we fear to do the dictates of our angels, and tremble at the tasks set before us; if we refuse to do spiritual acts because of natural fears or natural desires; who can describe the dismal torments of such a state! — I too well remember the threats I heard! — 'If you, who are organised by Divine Providence for Spiritual communion, refuse, and bury your talent in the earth, even though you should want natural bread, — sorrow and desperation pursue you through life, and after death shame and confusion of face to eternity!' "[1]

---

[1] *Letter to Butts*, Felpham, January 10, 1802.

Chapter III

WILLIAM BLAKE
1757—1827

SONGS OF INNOCENCE

My intention is to treat the most important of Blake's mystical works, those which are expressive of his most essential mystical vision. It is not so much my aim to give a complete exposition of his mystical writings as to draw from the principal ones that element which is the kernel of it. So it will be that many things, for instance most poems of the fine Rossetti-manuscript and many of the early prophecies are omitted, because their spirit was revealed elsewhere, or because I thought them of minor importance.

The first series of poems in which the mystic feeling of Blake found utterance is the *Songs of Innocence*. Never again was it to be expressed with such purity, such clarity and such tenderness as in these little gems of child-life. It is poetry abounding with all the sweets of earth and of Heaven. It is woven of sun-rays and infant-smiles, shining with the pure whiteness, the silent gleam of Him who put the child on the throne of humanity, when He declared it to be the possessor of the Heavenly Kingdom. The poet was completely immersed in the mystical profundity of Christ's vision of man's salvation through the impulsive innocence, the intuitive faith and trustful surrender of the child.

> "Piping down the valleys wild,
> Piping songs of pleasant glee,
> On a cloud I saw a child,
> And he laughing said to me:

'Pipe a song about a Lamb!'
So I piped with merry cheer.
'Piper, pipe that song again;'
So I piped: he wept to hear.

'Drop thy pipe, thy happy pipe;
Sing thy songs of happy cheer:'
So I sang the same again,
While he wept with joy to hear.

'Piper, sit thee down and write
In a book, that all may read.'
So he vanish'd from my sight,
And I pluck'd a hollow reed,

And I made a rural pen,
And I stain'd the water clear,
And I wrote my happy songs
Every child may joy to hear."

With this rippling melody he rang in his radiant vision of childhood, in which he found the treasures which the grown-up man may only possess in moments of deepest insight to be the child's natural dower. The babe of two days old has no feeling but joy, joy in the gift of life, of which it is yet unconscious.

'I have no name:
I am but two days old.'
What shall I call thee?
'I happy am,
Joy is my name.'
Sweet joy befall thee!

Pretty Joy!
Sweet Joy, but two days old.
Sweet Joy I call thee:
Thou dost smile,
I sing the while,
Sweet joy befall thee!"

How prettily expressive it is of the smiling happiness, the impulsive gladness of the little one. Like Shelley's skylark it is an embodied joy, darting its sparkles of luminous vitality like a halo around it, a sweet wonder of life, just blossomed forth, like a flower, from the bosom of God.

Afterwards we see it amidst the joyous sights and songs of spring playing on *The Echoing Green*, or we hear its exultant laugh amidst the laughter of hills and streams and groves. Then its joy is mingled with the joy of nature, which like the child's is impulsive, unconscious and without a shade of sorrow.

Another mystical atmosphere pervades *The Lamb*. The vision of exultant gladness is seen as through a veil. A tremulous tenderness of pious feeling lends to this little song a singular perfume of sanctity.

> "Little Lamb, who made thee?
> Dost thou know who made thee?
> Gave thee life, and bid thee feed,
> By the stream and o'er the mead;
> Gave thee clothing of delight,
> Softest clothing, woolly, bright;
> Gave thee such a tender voice,
> Making all the vales rejoice?
> Little Lamb, who made thee?
> Dost thou know who made thee?
>
> Little Lamb, I'll tell thee,
> Little Lamb, I'll tell thee:
> He is callèd by thy name,
> For He calls himself a Lamb.
> He is meek, and He is mild;
> He became a little child.
> I a child, and thou a lamb,
> We are callèd by His name,
> Little Lamb, God bless thee!
> Little Lamb, God bless thee!"

There is a spirit of devotional aspiration in it, a tone of meditative quiet, which is absent in the preceding songs. In the subtle symbolism by which the child and the lamb are exalted to the divinity of the Lamb of God and by which He stoops down to clothe himself in the sweet lowliness of earth's humble creatures, is enshrined the mystery of divine mercy. An even subtler and deeper feeling underlies the wonderfully tender *Cradle Song*, that marvel of grace and melody, fragile as gossamer, sweet as moonbeams, breathing the very peace of God that passeth all understanding.

"Sweet dreams, form a shade
O'er my lovely infant's head;
Sweet dreams of pleasant streams
By happy, silent, moony beams.

Sweet sleep, with soft down
Weave thy brows an infant crown.
Sweet sleep, Angel mild,
Hover o'er my happy child.

Sweet smiles, in the night
Hover over my delight;
Sweet smiles, mother's smiles,
All the livelong night beguiles.

Sweet moans, dovelike sighs,
Chase not slumber from thy eyes.
Sweet moans, sweeter smiles,
All the dovelike moans beguiles.

Sleep, sleep, happy child,
All creation slept and smil'd;
Sleep, sleep, happy sleep,
While o'er thee thy mother weep.

Sweet babe, in thy face
Holy image I can trace.
Sweet babe, once like thee,
Thy Maker lay and wept for me,

Wept for me, for thee, for all,
When He was an infant small.
Thou His image ever see,
Heavenly face that smiles on thee,

Smiles on thee, on me, on all:
Who became an infant small.
Infant smiles are His own smiles;
Heaven and earth to peace beguiles."

We see that an additional note is rung in this song, the note of human sorrow. We are farther advanced on the road of life, where the "still sad music of humanity" is heard amidst the joyous songs of the child's Eden. Speaking of poems like these Berger says: "Le paradis sans ombre de douleur ne semblerait pas complet: le poète veut encore pouvoir y ajouter le bonheur de la consolation divine. Cette dernière marque de l'amour divin aurait manqué s'il n'y avait point eu de chagrins à consoler. L'âge de l'innocence ne devrait point être celui des pleurs, en fait, il ne l'est que pour que ces pleurs puissent être immédiatement essuyés. Alors la douleur elle-même devient quelque chose de doux." [1]

As tender a devotion, and a still profounder sense of the need and of the certainty of redemption thrills in *On another's Sorrow*:

> "Can I see another's woe,
> And not be in sorrow too?
> Can I see another's grief,
> And not seek for kind relief?
>
> Can I see a falling tear,
> And not feel my sorrow's share?
> Can a father see his child
> Weep, nor be with sorrow fill'd?
>
> Can a mother sit and hear
> An infant groan, an infant fear?
> No, no! never can it be,
> Never, never can it be!

And can He who smiles on all
Hear the wren with sorrows small,
Hear the small bird's grief and care,
Hear the woes that infants bear,

And not sit beside the nest,
Pouring pity in their breast;
And not sit the cradle near,
Weeping tear on infant's tear;

And not sit both night and day,
Wiping all our tears away?
O, no! never can it be!
Never, never can it be!

He doth give His joy to all;
He becomes an infant small;
He becomes a man of woe;
He doth feel the sorrow too.

---

[1] Berger, *William Blake, etc.*, p. 347.

> Think not thou canst sigh a sigh,
> And thy Maker is not by;
> Think not thou canst weep a tear,
> And thy Maker is not near.
>
> O! He gives to us His joy
> That our grief He may destroy;
> Till our grief is fled and gone
> He doth sit by us and moan."

Divine love is ever near to take up the child in its protecting embrace. The little boy, who in the darkness of the lonely fen threatened to perish, experienced the saving presence of God, who, "ever nigh, appear'd like his father, in white."

> "He kissèd the child, and by the hand led,
> And to his mother brought,
> Who in sorrow pale, thro' the lonely dale,
> Her little boy weeping sought."

It is also the theme of *A Dream*, in which God leads His children home by the light of His love as the shining glow-worm does the emmet, lost in the darkness of the night. And this divine love may be revealed either directly, without any intermediary, or through man. Whenever a human creature is inspired by His spirit, Who is Love absolute, he will beam forth something of the supernal light on his fellow-men in distress:

> "To Mercy, Pity, Peace and Love
> All pray in their distress;
> And to these virtues of delight
> Return their thankfulness.
>
> For Mercy, Pity, Peace, and Love
> Is God, our Father dear,
> And Mercy, Pity, Peace, and Love
> Is man, His child and care.
>
> For Mercy has a human heart,
> Pity a human face,
> And Love the human form divine,
> And Peace, the human dress.
>
> Then every man, of every clime,
> That prays in his distress,
> Prays to the human form divine,
> Love, Mercy, Pity, Peace.

> And all must love the human form,
> In heathen, Turk, or Jew;
> Where Mercy, Love and Pity dwell
> There God is dwelling too." [1]

In this poem Blake shadows forth his later perplexing paradox from *The everlasting Gospel*:

> "Thou art a man, God is no more,
> Thy own humanity learn to adore," [2]

which in its semblance of blasphemy is the expression of his joyous knowledge of man being a partaker of the Divine Nature through the possession of Its very attributes, which all beam forth from the great central Light of Love.

An additional mystical note is heard in *Night*. We are carried beyond the Portal of Death into Life Eternal. The bright angels, who in the sleeping silence of the world, clothed in darkness, when the moon

> "like a flower
> In heaven's high bower,
> With silent delight
> Sits and smiles on the night,"

come pouring their sweet blessings on men, beasts and flowers, carry the golden keys of the gates of Immortal Life, where peace reigns supreme, where disharmony is solved into a higher unity, where the lion with his "ruddy eyes flowing with tears of gold," lies down beside the bleating lamb, thinking on the Saviour, and speaking the words of salvation:

> "Wrath, by his meekness,
> And by His health, sickness
> Is driven away
> From our immortal day."

In *The little black Boy* and in *The Chimney-Sweeper* we also find this belief in the true life after death, the belief that our sojourn on earth is only a prelude to the fullness of life after it,

---
[1] *The divine Image.*
[2] *The everlasting Gospel*, 75—77.

in God's radiant light of love, which in our weakness we could not yet bear.

> "And we are put on earth a little space,
> That we may learn to bear the beams of love;
> And these black bodies, and this sunburnt face
> Is but a cloud, and like a shady grove.
>
> For when our souls have learned the heat to bear,
> The cloud will vanish, we shall hear His voice,
> Saying: 'Come out from the grove, My Love and care,
> And round my golden tent like lambs rejoice.'" [1]

The angel who appears to the little chimney-sweeper in his dream, is evidently the angel of Death, proving to be the angel of Life, when he leads the little boys through the shadows of Death into eternal bliss. When, with a bright key, he has delivered them from their black coffins,

> "Then down a green plain leaping, laughing, they run,
> And wash in a river, and shine in the sun.
>
> Then naked and white, all their bags left behind,
> They rise upon clouds and sport in the wind."

Here Blake's later conception of life is the most strongly adumbrated, the conception, which sees in our earthly existence an imprisonment of the eternal spirit through the bodily bonds, created by Urizen, who separated himself from the world of the Eternals, to the full bliss of which man is only able to return through the Portal of Death. The little chimney-sweeper feels the chains of life laid very tightly and very heavily around him, but the bright vision of his dream and the angel's promise that

> "if he'd be a good boy,
> He'd have God for his father and never want joy,"

makes him do his earthly work in peace and happiness.

> "Tho' the morning was cold, Tom was happy and warm;
> So if all do their duty, they need not fear harm." [2]

---

[1] *The little black Boy.*
[2] *The Chimney-Sweeper.*

So faith and duty are considered in this song as life's saving powers. In this conception there is more of the full experience of the grown-up man, of his thoughtful resignation, of his hard-won hope, and faith born from tears, than in the other *Songs of Innocence*, with their impulsive joy and unclouded serenity; but yet through the whole atmosphere of the poem, fragrant with a singular perfume of innocence, childlike confidence and surrender, it is one of the brightest gems in the poet's vision of childhood.

With this poem we take leave of the *Songs of Innocence*, and it is with a feeling of tender sadness that we see the gates of Paradise shut upon us. This radiance of joy, this sweetness of consolation, this whiteness of innocence only belongs to the infancy of man, as it belonged to the infancy of humanity. When man has taken from the tree of knowledge of good and evil, the light of innocence is obscured by the experience of evil. On the horizon of his life he sees, looming up, dark and threatening, the clouds of law and division, obscuring God's joyous liberty and harmonious unity, which made his life such a sweet melody of spring, such a radiant vision of joy.

Chapter IV

SONGS OF EXPERIENCE

What this experience of life was for Blake is expressed in the whole sequel of his work with increasing obscurity, in proportion to a growing sense of the loss of liberty, which in the *Prophetic Books* became a veritable obsession to him.

Though chronologically the *Songs of Experience* are separated from the *Songs of Innocence* by a period of five years, in which *Thel, Tiriel,* the *Marriage of Heaven and Hell, Visions of the daughters of Albion, the Gates of Paradise* and *America* were written, yet they must be discussed in connection with these, because the two series form an indissoluble whole, in that they show life reflected in exactly opposite states of the soul. Blake himself combined them in one volume under the title of: *Songs of Innocence and Experience showing the two states of the human soul.*

The poems of the first part of the Rossetti Manuscript also belong to this period and reveal the same spirit.

In the *Introduction* we are immediately brought face to face with the poet's different attitude of mind. We breathe another spiritual atmosphere. The impulsive joy has given place to the dark brooding on the restraints of the spontaneous spirit of life. Instead of the joyous infant on the floating cloud, listening in rapt delight to the piper's happy melodies, we hear the voice of the Bard, the Seer, in whose mind the mysteries of Eternity are reflected, the Prophet, "who present, past and future sees," calling upon the soul of man to rise to her luminous heights of spiritual freedom, from which she has fallen into the abyss of tyrannical law. The whole earth groans under oppression now:

"O Earth, O Earth, return!
Arise from out the dewy grass;

> Night is worn.
> And the morn
> Rises from the slumberous mass.
>
> Turn away no more,
> Why wilt thou turn away.
> The starry floor,
> The wat'ry shore,
> Is giv'n thee till the break of day."

Berger understood the last lines to mean that the beauties of nature, which remind man of eternity, will be his till the day of the resurrection, when bondage and division shall be solved into freedom and unity. Is he not able, before the breaking of that day, to tear himself loose from the forces that chain him, the Bard asks in urgent appeal, to which we hear Earth's despondent answer that she cannot deliver herself from the bonds which restrain her natural impulses. Social and religious laws stifle in her the spirit of life, which is embodied in the Bard.

Foster Damon explains "the starry floor" as "Reason, roofing Man in from Eternity," "the wat'ry shore" as "the dead Sea of Time and Space." [2] I should think the first explanation the most poetical, doing most justice to the possible artistic conception of the poet, the latter may be more correct in the light of Blake's mystical symbolism, which he developed more completely in the *Prophetic Books*.

To a great extent the *Songs of Experience* still sing of children. But instead of the blue Heavens arching in ever-luminous radiance of joy over the child's Paradise, instead of its blessed existence, steeped in the grand sweetness of divine consolation, translucent with the eternal Sun of heavenly Love, there is an obscure atmosphere here, veiling the effulgence of the blue expanse, hiding the world of Eternity, which the child in its freedom of soul unconsciously adumbrated behind the far horizons that stretched in unclouded serenity before its enraptured gaze. The disembodied spirit, the pure essence of life which let itself float on the impulse of divine inspiration, has been fettered. A shimmering of pathetic fragility and defenceless innocence gleams through this poetry, a

[1] Berger, *William Blake, etc.*, p. 357.
[2] Foster Damon, *William Blake, etc.*, p. 274.

spirit of deep compassion, in which is felt the symbolical depth of the soul of man pursued by antagonistic forces, innocence crucified. Individual experience is widened into a universal process. Experience makes the child look with bitterness on the sorrows that cloud its young existence, on the dangers that lurk all around.

> "My mother groan'd, my father wept,
> Into the dangerous world I leapt;
> Helpless, naked, piping loud,
> Like a fiend hid in a cloud.
>
> Struggling in my father's hands,
> Striving against my swaddling-bands,
> Bound and weary, I thought best
> To sulk upon my mother's breast." [1]

The Chimney-Sweeper's bright vision of joy is obscured by the laws of religion, which, made by the hand of man, and ignoring God, kill the flaming vitality of his little soul.

> "A little black thing among the snow,
> Crying 'weep! weep!' in notes of woe!
> 'Where are thy father and mother, say?'
> 'They are both gone up to the Church to pray.
>
> Because I was happy upon the heath,
> And smil'd among the winter's snow,
> They cloth'd me in the clothes of death,
> And taught me to sing the notes of woe.
>
> 'And because I am happy and dance and sing,
> They think they have done me no injury,
> And are gone to praise God and His Priest and King,
> Who make up a Heaven of our misery.'"

And *The little Vagabond* cannot go to church, because he feels its coldness, its lack of life. The ale-house, with its congenial warmth, its happy atmosphere, is a place where his soul finds a better soil to grow in according to its congenital nature.

> "But if at the Church they would give us some ale,
> And a pleasant fire our souls to regale,
> We'd sing and we'd pray all the livelong day,
> Nor ever once wish from the Church to stray."

---

[1] *Infant Sorrow.*

Then the children would be as happy as birds in the spring and God Himself would rejoice because of his children's rejoicing and He would love the Devil as being the Distributor of this rippling merriment.

How different are the *Holy Thursday* of the Songs of Innocence and this one. There a sweet naive vision of the children singing joyous hymns of praise to God, like angels adoring, here the trembling cry of the infants reduced to physical and spiritual starvation.

> "Is this a holy thing to see
> In a rich and fruitful land,
> Babes reduc'd to misery,
> Fed with cold and usurous hand?
>
> Is that trembling cry a song?
> Can it be a song of joy?
> And so many children poor?
> It is a land of poverty!
>
> And their sun does never shine,
> And their fields are bleak and bare,
> And their ways are fill'd with thorns:
> It is eternal winter there.
>
> For where'er the sun does shine,
> And where'er the rain does fall,
> Babe can never hunger there,
> Nor poverty the mind appal."

Like the church, like the community, the school is an oppressive force in the child's life. Instead of enjoying the glad songs of a summer morning, instead of mingling its joy with the joy of nature, whose impulsive life it essentially shares, it is imprisoned like a bird in a cage and forgets its songs of happy liberty and droops its tender wings that carried it in mystical flight through the gladsome air beyond the bourns of time and space.

> "How can the bird that is born for joy
> Sit in a cage and sing?
> How can a child, when fears annoy,
> But droop his tender wing,
> And forget his youthful spring?"

And anticipating disconsolate years of barren existence he calls out in pathetic helplessness:

> "O! father and mother, if buds are nipp'd
> And blossoms blown away,
> And if the tender plants are stripp'd
> Of their joy in the springing day,
> By sorrow and care's dismay,
>
> How shall the summer arise in joy,
> Or the summer fruits appear?
> Or how shall we gather what griefs destroy,
> Or bless the mellowing year,
> When the blasts of winter appear?"

Whereas the sleeping babe had been immersed in the profoundness of a sweet and serene tranquillity with the gleam of God's smile hovering protectingly round, it is now disturbed by little sorrows and soft desires. The sweetness of heavenly peace in its golden purity is gone. The crystalline radiance of dawn has faded.

The vision of the Lamb hovers no longer in the poet's mind as the symbol of the godlike purity of life's essential spirit, but the splendid terror of the tiger has thrust upon him other and fiercer aspects of creation.

> "Tiger! Tiger! burning bright
> In the forests of the night,
> What immortal hand or eye
> Could frame thy fearful symmetry?
>
> In what distant deeps or skies
> Burnt the fire of thine eyes?
> On what wings dare he aspire?
> What the hand dare seize the fire?
>
> And what shoulder, and what art,
> Could twist the sinews of thy heart?
> And when thy heart began to beat,
> What dread hand? and what dread feet?
>
> What the hammer? what the chain?
> In what furnace was thy brain?
> What the anvil? what dread grasp
> Dare its deadly terrors clasp?" etc.

This poem is one of the most powerful and almost unique among Blake's lyrical songs in its flaming energy, its rich colouring, its sweeping transport of passion.

"Even in Blake's own day, when most of his poems were quite unknown, this one was circulated everywhere, for it was unforgettable. It was the first thing that Lamb ever heard of Blake's: 'I have heard of his poems, but have never seen them. There is one to a tiger.... which is glorious!'" [1]

What is peculiarly Blakean, and what we shall see expressed again and again, is his conception of God as a Man, [2] as it is for instance expressed in the *Auguries of Innocence*.

> "God appears and God is Light
> To those poor souls who dwell in Night,
> But does a Human Form display
> To those who dwell in realms of Day."

Connecting this with the vision which sees in the fly a man like himself and in himself a fly, together with the paradoxical statement in *The Everlasting Gospel*: "Thou art a man, God is no more," we come to the core of Blake's belief that the whole of the visible creation is one manifestation in different forms of one Spirit, the Spirit of Man, which is also the spirit of God, only discernible by that Spirit, the human-divine Imagination.

It is very noteworthy that Blake, the enthusiastic fighter for the life of the spirit, should symbolise his conception of God's immanence in the human form. No one, perhaps, has insisted so strongly on the spirit being the only reality and no one perhaps has materialized so much his spiritual visions in tangible forms.

Like man's the fly's natural joy is stifled:

> "Little Fly,
> Thy summer's play
> My thoughtless hand
> Has brush'd away.

---

[1] Foster Damon, *William Blake, etc.*, p. 276, quoted from *Gilchrist, The Life of William Blake*, ch. XIII.
[2] See page 21.

>   Am not I
>   A fly like thee?
>   Or art not thou
>   A man like me?
>
>   For I dance,
>   And drink, and sing
>   Till some blind hand
>   Shall brush my wing.
>
>   If thought is life
>   And strength and breath,
>   And the want
>   Of thought is death;
>
>   Then am I
>   A happy fly,
>   If I live
>   Or if I die."

Love, too, is fettered by laws. Whilst nature may live according to her innate impulses, man is bound by the chain of reason and external decency. Earth's answer to the Ancient Bard is a cry of despair and an appeal for help:

> "Does spring hide its joy
> When birds and blossoms grow?
> Does the sower
> Sow by night,
> Or the ploughman in darkness plough?
>
> Break this heavy chain
> That does freeze my bones around.
> Selfish! vain!
> Eternal bane!
> That free Love with bondage bound."

The same theme is treated of in *The Garden of Love*, which blossoms no longer in the luxury of its early delight, having its sweet flowers killed by pharisaical priests, so that instead of rejoicing life we see the death-like grey of tomb-stones.

In a world like this man is no longer the pure image of divine love, but cruelty and deceit have deformed his godlike countenance. He has wandered away far from the Light and it is in the intense feeling of the loss of life's brightest treasure that the poet turns to *Tirzah*, "the mother of his mortal part," she who bound him with the bodily bonds, reproaching her with the curse that has fallen on him:

> "Thou, Mother of my mortal part,
> With cruelty didst mould my heart,
> And with false, self-deceiving tears
> Didst bind my nostrils, eyes and ears;
>
> Didst close my tongue in senseless clay
> And me to mortal life betray,"

after which suddenly the poet rises to the mystic heights of pure insight where he is loosened from the bonds of matter.

> "The death of Jesus set me free:
> Then what have I to do with thee?"

"Blake undoubtedly wrote this poem when trying to interpret the unfilial remark of the child Jesus in the Temple: 'Woman, what have I to do with thee?' (John II, 4) Blake's conclusion was that Jesus was interrupted in his consideration of spiritual matters by the intrusion of her who bound him into the corporeal world. This is the case with every man. For the mortal body is of the earth, and will return to it, a temporary delusion, the true body is the spiritual body: a distinction made by Paul (1 Cor. XV, 44) which is quoted by Blake in the marginal decoration to this poem. The sexes were therefore produced by the Fall, and in Eternity will vanish.... But Mercy (Jesus) turned this Death from Eternity into a sleep — we shall awake again. Jesus himself descended to show us the way back: his own "death" has set us free from these delusions.
'Then what have I to do with thee,' the continuer of them?" [1]

Berger thinks Blake alludes to the resurrection after the death of the body in Christ. I am inclined to think that Blake's symbolism may enclose both the salvation through Christ after death and in this life. In *Jerusalem* Blake said: "I know of no other Christi-

---

[1] Foster Damon, *William Blake, etc.*, p. 281.

anity and of no other Gospel than the liberty both of body and mind to exercise the Divine Arts of Imagination — Imagination, the real and Eternal World of which this Vegetable Universe is but a faint shadow. What is Immortality, but the things relating to the Spirit, which lives eternally," etc.

In connexion with Blake's belief in Christ's redeeming power I would point out that it was a belief in a purely spiritual regeneration. The doctrine of atonement was odious to him. Crabb Robinson reports his having said on this subject: "Atonement? It is a horrible doctrine. If another man pay your debt, I do not forgive it." [1]

The two poems which next call for our attention are *The little Girl lost* and *The little Girl found*. Whereas *To Tirzah* is a typical specimen of his later poetry, both in the spirit of it and in its language, which gives a premonition of his future obscure symbolism, these hark back to the time of his first inspiration. Indeed, they were included in the early issues of the *Songs of Innocence*, but were transferred by Blake to the *Songs of Experience* on the completion of the latter.

Lyca, the little girl, who, wandering, listened to the wild birds' song, got lost in the desert, where she fell asleep, and where she was found by the wild beasts, who, full of tender care, conveyed her to their caves. When her parents, anxious and sad, because of the loss of their little girl, went out in the night to seek her, they were met on the road by a couching lion, which was transfigured before their eyes into a spirit "armed in gold," bringing comfort and help, instead of terror.

> "On his head a crown;
> On his shoulders down
> Flow'd his golden hair.
> Gone was all their care.
>
> 'Follow me', he said:
> 'Weep not for the maid;
> In my palace deep
> Lyca lies asleep.'

---

[1] Crabb Robinson, *Diary*, December, 1826.

> Then they followèd
> Where the vision led,
> And saw their sleeping child
> Among tigers wild.
>
> To this day they dwell
> In a lonely dell;
> Nor fear the wolfish howl
> Nor the lions' growl."

We recognize in this lion the one of the *Songs of Innocence* with "the ruddy eyes flowing with tears of gold." The wandering of the little girl is a symbolical representation of the girl's earthly life, her sleep is the sleep of death, and the Lion represents divine protection and love, which at she same time is the Angel of Death.

However critics may judge of Blake's so-called *Prophetic Books*, they nearly all of them agree that he was very great in these little songs. Swinburne, the enthusiastic eulogist of the whole of Blake's poetical work, to whom the honour is due of having been the first after Gilchrist to draw the attention to the great beauty of Blake's poetry, speaks in words of devout rapture about these songs. He is the only one who distinctly states his preference for the *Songs of Experience* to the *Songs of Innocence*. "Against all articulate authority," he says, "we class several of the *Songs of Experience* higher for the great qualities of verse than anything in the earlier division of these poems. If the *Songs of Innocence* have the shape and smell of leaves or buds, these have in them the light and sound of fire or the sea. Entering among them, a fresher savour and a larger breath strikes one upon the lips and forehead. In the first part we are shown who they are who have or who deserve the gift of spiritual sight: in the second what things there are for them to see when that gift has been given. Innocence, the quality of beasts and children, has the keenest eyes; and such eyes alone can discern and interpret the actual mysteries of experience. It is natural that this second part, dealing as it does with such things as underlie the outer forms of the first part, should rise higher and dive deeper in point of mere words."[1] I cannot agree with Swinburne's opinion. The first part stands on a higher

---

[1] Swinburne, *William Blake*, p. 127.

mystic level than the second. The latter, as expressive of a state of the mind through which man has to pass after the golden dream of his childhood, when life's conflicting forces come rushing in upon him, may be maturer as to experience of the whole of human life, it may command a wider range of perception, but from a mystical and poetical point of view it is not deeper. In the *Songs of Innocence* the poet revealed the glory of a life which is free from the oppression of material conditions. If man shall live again the child's God-possessed existence he has to become as one of them.

"Verily, I say unto you, except ye be converted and become as little children, ye shall not enter into the Kingdom of Heaven." [1]

Suffer the little children to come unto me, and forbid them not: for of such is the kingdom of God." [2]

It is because they are inspired by the tender and holy wisdom of these Gospel-words, which Blake in the transforming power of his poetic and mystic genius presents to us with the freshness of a new creation that they touch the secret of life, that they are among the most purely mystical songs in English literature.

Berger says of the *Songs of Innocence and Experience*: "Ces Chants sont réellement l'oeuvre poétique par excellence de Blake, celle où il est exquis et parfait. Ce sont eux qui ont attiré l'attention sur lui et qui l'ont fait classer parmi les grands poètes. C'est probablement par eux seuls qu'il vivra dans l'histoire de la poésie anglaise. Chez aucun autre la même note ne se fera entendre, parce que nulle part ne se retrouvera un poète d'une foi telle qu'il ait pu ressusciter en lui l'âme simple d'un enfant et d'un mysticisme tel qu'il ait pu vivre complètement dans l'Eden de ses rêves et ne voir le monde comme pourrait le voir un ange égaré parmi nous." [3] I venture the remark that the *Songs of Innocence* were uppermost in his mind, when he wrote these words of admiring appreciation.

---

[1] *St. Matthew* XVIII, 23.
[2] *St. Mark* X, 14.
[3] Berger, *William Blake, etc.*, p. 374.

CHAPTER V

SOME EARLY PROPHETIC BOOKS

Blake's *Prophetic Books* may be divided into two parts, the early and shorter prophecies, those which he made from 1789 to 1796, and his later and longer ones. [1]

The first of the Prophetic Books, *Thel*, stands on the boundary of the two spiritual spheres which we can trace in Blake's poetry. On the one hand there is still the radiance of youth, on the other hand we have the gloom of advanced life that darkens its light.

For the greater part its thought and style are lucid, but beginnings of an obscure symbolism show themselves.

Thel, the youngest of the daughters of the Seraphim, has separated herself from her sisters and sits down by the river of Adona. She feels sad, because her life is destined to fade away. The feeling of transitoriness weighs her down heavily and thus "her gentle lamentation falls like morning-dew:"

"O life of this our spring! why fades the lotus of the water?
Why fade these children of the spring, born but to smile and fall?
Ah! Thel is like a wa'try bow, and like a parting cloud,
Like a reflection in a glass, like shadows in the water,
Like dreams of infants, like a smile upon an infant's face,
Like the dove's voice, like transient day, like music in the air.
Ah! gentle may I lay me down and gentle rest my head,
And gentle sleep the sleep of death, and gentle hear the voice
Of him that walketh in the garden in the evening time." [2]

Then the tender and lowly things of nature come to her to speak

[1] His early prophecies are: *Thel, Tiriel, The Marriage of Heaven and Hell, The French Revolution, Song of Liberty, Visions of the Daughters of Albion, America, Europe, The Book of Urizen, The Book of Los, The Book of Ahania, The Song of Los*. His later prophecies are: *The four Zoa's* (partly), *Milton* and *Jerusalem*.
[2] *Thel* I, 6—15.

words of solace. The lily of the valley, which likes to live unobserved in the humble grass and which is so weak that the gilded butterfly can scarcely perch upon its head, is happy, because she knows herself to be visited by God.

> "he that smiles on all
> Walks in the valley, and each morn over me spreads his hand,
> Saying: 'Rejoice, thou humble grass, thou new-born lily-flower,
> Thou gentle maid of silent valleys and of modest brooks.'" [1]

What makes her life also happy is the knowledge of being a blessing to earth's humble creatures which live unobserved and in silent endurance, to "those that cannot crave, the voiceless, the o'ertired." But Thel cannot be comforted. She compares herself to a faint cloud kindled at the rising sun and vanishing from her pearly throne without leaving a trace. Then the lily of the valley calls down the little cloud from its glittering throne in the morning-sky to bring her soothing message of consolation to the despairing seraph. "O maid," she says,

> "I tell thee, when I pass away,
> It is to tenfold life, to love, to peace and raptures holy." [2]

Dissolving she will appear as morning dew upon balmy flowers, thus giving her life for the benefit of others and in doing so fulfilling life's sacred law.

> "everything that lives
> Lives not alone nor for itself." [3]

The wisdom of these words the little cloud instills into the disconsolate heart of the seraph-child. But still Thel cannot be comforted. She does not see the use of her bright existence, which is to end in the darkness of the grave, a prey to the worms that destroy. Then the clod of clay, symbol of death's destructive power, sings its joyous song of faith and hope. It repeats the cloud's wisdom:

[1] *Thel* I, 19—23.
[2] *Ibid.* II, 10—12.
[3] *Ibid.*, 26—27.

SOME EARLY PROPHETIC BOOKS 37

"O beauty of the vales of Har, we live not for ourselves.
Thou seest me, the meanest thing, and so I am indeed,
My bosom of itself is cold, and of itself is dark;
But he that loves the lowly, pours his oil upon my head
And kisses me, and binds his nuptial bands around my breast,
And says: 'Thou mother of my children, I have loved thee,
And I have given thee a crown that none can take away.'
But how this is, sweet maid, I know not, and I cannot know,
I ponder, and I cannot ponder; yet I live and love." [1]

This humble clod of clay has the key to the reality of life. It is consoled by God's mercy and therefore it is happy and lives a beautiful life of sacrificial love. It accepts the precious gift of divine consolation without understanding its mystery and in this very absence of understanding lies the wisdom of God.

At last Thel is admitted into the domain of death, where she visits her own grave, from which she hears these words of sorrow breathed forth:

"Why cannot the Ear be closed to its own destruction,
Or the glist'ning Eye to the poison of a smile?
Why are Eyelids stor'd with arrows ready drawn
Where a thousand fighting men in ambush lie;
Or an Eye of gifts and graces show'ring fruits and coined gold?
Why a Tongue impress'd with honey from every wind?
Why an Ear, a whirlpool fierce to draw creations in?
Why a Nostril wide inhaling terror, trembling and affright?
Why a tender curb upon the youthful, burning boy?
Why a little curtain of flesh on the bed of our desire?" [2]

When Thel heard these gloomy words she

"started from her seat, and with a shriek
Fled back unhinder'd till she came into the vales of Har." [3]

Swinburne thinks that Thel's death represents the death of the physical body. "In this book," he says, "as in the illustrations to Blair, the poet attempts to comfort life through death; to assuage by spiritual hope the fleshly fear of man. The "shining woman" feeds upon the sorrow that comes of beauty, the heathen weariness of heart, that is sick of life because death will come, seeing how

[1] *Thel* III, 10—19.
[2] *Ibid.* IV, 11—21.
[3] *Ibid.*, 21—22.

"our little life is rounded with a sleep." [1] Berger sees a different meaning in the poem. He is of opinion that Thel's death represents the birth of the body, the fettering of the spirit. "Thel est la fille des séraphins, un esprit immortel, qui va bientôt être enfermé dans l'argile morte, être végété, naître à la terre, devenir une âme humaine douée d'un corps." [2] He thinks, that the scene of this poem is laid in two regions: in the realm of Eternity, the dwelling-place of Thel, and in the land of mortal existence, the place where the cloud, the lily of the valley, the worm and the clod live. Foster Damon also sees in the death of Thel the formation of the physical body. I cannot but feel in the poem, at least partly, a lament at the transitoriness of life. The following lines speak in favour of this conception.

"she in paleness sought the secret air,
To fade away like morning beauty from her *mortal day*." [3]

"Why fade these children of the spring, *born* but to smile and fall?" [4]

"For thou shalt be clothed in light, and fed with morning manna
Till summer's heat melts thee beside the fountains and the springs
To flourish in *eternal vales*." [5]

"Did she only live to be *at death the food of worms ?*" [6]

The last section may be the expression of the tragedy of mortal life, as already experienced by Thel, but it seems very probable to me that a double symbolism hovered in the poet's mind here. I believe that Berger and Foster Damon's conception of Thel's death representing the emprisonment of the spirit in the body, when applied to the lament at the end: "Why cannot the Ear be closed to its own destruction, etc., is correct, especially when we consider that it may be a later addition. [7]

But whatever may be its exact meaning, it is one of the finest

---

[1] Swinburne, *William Blake*, p. 222.
[2] Berger, *William Blake*, etc., pp. 382, 383.
[3] *Thel* I, 2—4.
[4] *Ibid.*, 7.
[5] *Ibid.* II, 23—25.
[6] *Ibid.* II, 23.
[7] See Sloss and Wallis, vol. II, p. 267.

poems written by Blake. In its tender sweetness and pathetic grief it is most appealing. We have here still much of the purity, the clarity of vision and diction, which distinguishes many of his early lyrics, the atmosphere is not yet loaded with the weighty broodings of gloomy mysticism. Notwithstanding its tone of bitter sadness, it is still luminous with the charm of his early vision, the child of the *Songs of Innocence* still adorns it with its grace and loveliness. Its simple and spontaneous faith, which accepts with devotional surrender without questioning, still endows it with its mystic gleam.

In *The Marriage of Heaven and Hell*, which Swinburne, with some exaggerated praise, calls the greatest of all Blake's books, a work which he ranks as about the greatest produced by the eighteenth century in the line of high poetry and spiritual speculation, we find for the first time set forth most of Blake's later perplexing mystical conceptions, with an imaginative force, an atmospheric magic, a fervour of passion, which is fascinating and at the same time startling in its grotesque obscurity and paradoxical eccentricity. [1]

The first doctrine set forth in this strange and weird medley of heavenly and hellish wisdom is that of a divine unity underlying the diversity of appearances. Blake sings about the Marriage of Heaven and Hell, as the unity of opposite principles. They are necessary in the great purpose of life.

"Without Contraries is no progression.
Attraction and Repulsion, Reason and Energy, Love and Hate, are necessary to Human existence." [2]

And everything that lives is holy. In this *Proverb of Hell* we have in epitome the spiritual essence of *The Marriage*, which is a glowing panegyric of life, and therefore a fierce denunciation of those powers that restrain it.

"The pride of the peacock is the glory of God.
The lust of the goat is the bounty of God.
The wrath of the lion is the wisdom of God.
The nakedness of woman is the work of God." [3]

Social and religious conventionalism, symbolised in the angels,

---
[1] Its beginnings are to be traced in the preceding poems.
[2] *The Argument.*
[3] *Proverbs of Hell.*

condemn these divine gifts. Therefore Blake is on the side of the devil, who lives unrestrained, according to his innate impulses. Evil does not exist, only in the form of restraint of energy, which is "eternal delight."

The Devil is heard to say:

"All Bibles or sacred codes have been the causes of the following errors:
1. That Man has two real existing principles, Viz. a Body and a Soul.
2. That Energy, call'd Evil, is alone from the Body; and that Reason, call'd Good, is alone from the Soul.
3. That God will torment Man in Eternity for following his Energies.
But the following Contraries to these are True:
1. Man has no Body distinct from his Soul; for that call'd Body is a portion of Soul discern'd by the five Senses, the chief inlets of Soul in this age.
2. Energy is the only life, and is from the Body; and Reason is the bound or outward circumference of Energy.
3. Energy is Eternal Delight." [1]

Walking among the fires of Hell, delighted with the enjoyments of Genius, which to Angels look like torment and insanity, the poet collected some proverbs, a few of which I quoted, and which belong to the finest part of his speculative poetry. Some of them also give expression to this passionate belief in the freeness of the spirit.

"The road of excess leads to the palace of wisdom."
"He who desires but acts not breeds pestilence."
"Sooner murder an infant in its cradle than nurse unacted desires." [2]

Blake's Christianity had not yet attained the height which it reached in the later prophetic books, where the doctrine of forgiveness of sins was held out by him as the greatest Christian revelation.

"The cut worm forgives the plow."
"A dead body revenges not injuries." [3]

Hate is still part of the doctrine of energy. Kassner and Symons drew attention to Blake's spiritual relationship with Nietzsche.

"Man must become better and wickeder. Everyman must find his own virtue." [4]

[1] *The voice of the Devil.*
[2] *Proverbs of Hell.*
[3] *Ibid.*
[4] Nietzsche, *Zarathustra*, quoted by Symons, *William Blake*, p. 2.

The doctrine of liberty, which is apt to be a very dangerous one, is sanctioned by the Bible. "Where the Spirit of the Lord is there is Liberty," St. Paul says, but I doubt very much if Blake's mentality when he wrote *the Marriage* was the same as St. Paul's!

In connection with Blake's belief in absolute moral freedom Swinburne says:

"Translated into rough practice, and planted in a less pure soil than that of the writer's mind, this philosophy might bring forth a strange harvest." [1] Of Jesus, to Blake the highest type of humanity, he says: "Jesus was all virtue, and acted from impulse, not from rules." Therefore he denounces the ten commandments as being in contradiction with the very principle of life, and then tries, with forced argument, to indicate that Christ acted in opposition to them.

His belief in divine immanence finds again and again expression in the most startling paradoxical heresies:

"The worship of God is: Honouring his gifts in other men, each according to his genius, and loving the greatest men best: those who envy or calumniate great men hate God; for there is no other God." [2]
"Men forgot that All Deities reside in the human breast." [3]
"God only Acts and Is, in existing beings or Men." [4]

When Isaiah said that God spoke to him "he did not see Him or hear Him in a finite organical perception", but, he says:

"My senses discover'd the infinite in every thing." [5]

Another belief which Blake holds is that the spiritual world is only partly accessible to man, a finite being, bound by the senses, "the chief inlets of soul." When man shall have done away with these and appear in his original state of freedom at the end of six thousand years, when, according to the ancient tradition, the world will be consumed by fire,

[1] Swinburne, *William Blake*, p. 230.
[2] *A Memorable Fancy.*
[3] *Proverbs of Hell.*
[4] *A Memorable Fancy.*
[5] *Ibid.*

"the whole creation will appear infinite and holy, whereas it now appears finite and corrupt."

"If the doors of perception were cleansed, everything would appear to man as it is, infinite."

"For man has closed himself up, till he sees all things thro' narrow chinks of his cavern."
"How do you know but ev'ry Bird that cuts the airy way,
Is an immense world of delight, clos'd by your senses five?"[1]

And the great force which lifts man to the high level of mystical insight is the poetic genius, the imaginative power, the religious inspiration, all arising from the same divine source, identical in essence.

> "What is now proved was once only imagin'd."
> "One thought fills immensity."
> "Everything possible to be believ'd is an image of truth."[2]

In these fine and suggestive lines, which open to the human mind the hidden possibilities of infinity, we have in a nutshell Blake's passionate belief in the supreme power of the imagination, which henceforth was to be the chief inspiring force of his work.

---

[1] *A Memorable Fancy.*
[2] *Proverbs of Hell.*

CHAPTER VI

THE FALL

The symbolism which we could detect in the *Songs of Innocence*, which showed itself stronger in the *Songs of Experience*, which was to be seen in *Thel*, which also to a great extent is the form in which the thought of the *Marriage of Heaven and Hell* is clothed, became afterwards almost the only vehicle in which Blake expressed his thought.

Symbolism is the medium through which the mystic often expresses himself. Because he wants to sing about the eternal essence, which is invisible to the physical eye, a natural vehicle will be a language which in its imagery suggests the reality which is revealed to him. "Allegory addressed to the intellectual powers, while it is altogether hidden from the corporeal understanding, is my definition of the most sublime poetry," said Blake in a letter to Butts [1].

In his later *Proheptic Books* Blake developed an entire symbolical system, in which the wonderful world which opened to the seer is revealed to us, a world weird and dim, far away from the earth on which we live, and yet often tied to it by unbreakable bonds of spiritual union, a world in which we often feel strangers, forlorn, at a loss to find our way, but which at times holds us in its grasp, because in the mysterious phantom-figures that are born and die, move and live, suffer and rejoice in that remote land of glimmering dreams, we recognize the bearers of the great forces of humanity. [2]

---

[1] R. L. Nettleship says: "True mysticism is the consciousness that everything that we experience is an element, and only an element in fact, i. e. that in being what it is it is s y m b o l i c of something more." (Inge, *Christian Mysticism*, p. 342.)

[2] In connection with Blake's symbolism it will be adequate to quote a statement from the Preface to Russel and Maclagan's edition of the *Prophetic Books*: "It can hardly be supposed that each line of the *Prophetic Books*

I have drawn attention to the fact that what the mystic sees is that diversity and contrariety are not the inner facts of the universe, that they are solved into a harmonious unity in the life of things. This unity Blake saw gleaming in a vision, where man slept in the bosom of Eternity. There was no time, no space, because eternity was all, and man was taken up in its spaceless omnipresence. [1]

It was before the creation of the world.

> "Earth was not, nor globes of attraction;
> The will of the Immortal expanded
> Or contracted his all-flexible senses;
> Death was not, but eternal life sprung." [2]

It was life, pristine and pure, in which earthly man still stands rooted.

Then "a shadow of horror" rose in eternity, "unknown, unprolific, self-closed, all-repelling", a shadow that "divided times on times and measured space by space" in his darkness. The appearance of this shadow, whose name is Urizen, was the beginning of creation, which is division in the divine unity. And at the same time when the unity broke up, time was born. Time, in the mythological figure of Los, the creator of the Sun, solidified in his furnaces of fire the floating, changing forms of the shadowy stature which divided itself from the world of eternal life. The latter became enclosed within the prison-house of his five senses, [3] his "fountain of thought" was shut up in the barring solidity of the body, till the glory of his home was lost as the beautiful vision of a dream. Therefore he was inwardly torn by anguish and his terrible groans of dismay were heard over the nether Abyss and his giant-form expanded as an all-predominating power in space.

will ever be interpreted in a manner entirely satisfying. Nor can a simple significance be attached to each symbol by which it may be translated, in whatever context it may occur, for symbolism, whether it be that of Ezekiel or of the Apocalypse, of Dante or of Blake, necessarily deals with truths too universal to be comprehended in a literal formula and confounds the commentator by its infinite application."

[1] See Kassner, *die Mystik, die Künstler und das Leben*, p. 62.
[2] *Urizen* II, 1—5.
[3] Swinburne thinks that these transformations of Urizen make up some of Blake's grandest and strangest prophetic studies. (*William Blake*, p. 274.)

> "Enraged and stifled with torment,
> He threw his right Arm to the north,
> His left Arm to the south,
> Shooting out in anguish deep;
> And his Feet stamp'd the nether Abyss
> In trembling and howling and dismay." [1]

Thus the figure of Urizen is the symbolical representation of visible creation. He is the universal world of matter. But he is also the materialistic part in man, his reasoning, analytical, dissecting faculty, which is engrossed by things temporal, as distinguished from his godlike imagination, on whose wings he is carried to eternity's luminous heights. So the Macrocosm is mirrored in the Microcosm and conversely. It was not that Blake saw an evil power in reason in itself, but in reason, when it leaves its own place in creation and tries to usurp the kingdom of the universal Spirit, called by him Urthona,[2] so reason, the stifler of inspiration, of natural life, of natural joys, of innocent love, reason, as it weaves the cold and dark web of religion, so strong in its "twisted cords and knotted meshes", that imagination cannot break it through.

It is reason that sets up one law for the infinite variety of life's revelations, Urizen, who reads his laws from the Book of Eternal Brass, written in his solitude of dark contemplation.

> "Laws of peace, of love, of unity,
> Of pity, compassion, forgiveness.
> Let each chuse one habitation,
> His ancient infinite mansion,
> One command, one joy, one desire,
> One curse, one weight, one measure,
> One King, one God, one Law." [3]

Urizen wanted to enforce by law that which can only exist by its own living fullness. He did not see that peace, love, unity, pity, compassion, forgiveness, are life itself, only real, when spontaneous, vital, and hot with the fervour of individual conviction and experience and otherwise nothing but a mocking mask concealing death. Thus Urizen also stands for dogma, dead formulism in religion.

---

[1] *Book of Urizen* IV, 82—88.
[2] In *The four Zoas* the tragedy of Urizen's usurping tendency is treated of at large.
[3] The *Book of Urizen* II, 43—50.

> "Eternity stood wide apart,
> As the stars are apart from the earth." [1]

The six ages which it took Los to accomplish his task are symbolically related to the Biblical six days of creation. To Blake, as to the Swedish seer Swedenborg, whose influence he underwent, the Bible was the bearer of the symbol of the universal and of the individual life of man. Much of its hidden, spiritual meaning was revealed by Blake in the bulk of his art. The mystical Paradise of Innocence, in which Adam and Eve lived in the light of God's love before the fall is Blake's world before the universe rose in blinding, darkening opacity on the light of the deep. Their fall is the fall of Urizen from eternity into time, from spirit into matter. Afterwards we shall see that part of Urizen is separated from him. [2] It is the female Ahania. This is the symbolical representation of the division of man into sexes. In the mystical paradise man was sexless, which Christ expressed by the words: "In the resurrection they neither marry nor are given in marriage." But we must not forget that this obvious symbolism may also hide the deeper meaning, the fall from divine unity. With Blake we often find symbol within symbol, reaching through outer covering to the core of things.

Urizen, exploring the regions of his new-created world, saw his world "teeming with frightful, vast, enormous portions of life," he saw that the fearful work of creation that had been enacted in him was repeated everywhere. The victims of his fall "shrunk up six days from existence."

> "And on the seventh day they rested,
> And they bless'd the seventh day in sick hope,
> And forgot their eternal life." [3]

We here recognize the Biblical six days of creation.

Los, realising the sadness of Urizen's fate, felt Pity stirring within him. She separated herself from Los, and Enitharmon, the first female was born. She is also space, who together with time, has its being in creation and creation in them. We find here symbolised the statement of Jacob Boehme, who was one of Blake's spiritual masters, that "creation is the introduction of space and time into the world of individual wills". [4]

[1] *The Book of Urizen* III, 49—51.
[2] *The Book of Ahania.*
[3] *The Book of Urizen* IX, 17—20.
[4] See Berger, *William Blake, etc.*, p. 118.

In connection with Blake's conception of the creation it will be adequate to quote Foster Damon: "Blake seems to have rediscovered, or perhaps adopted for himself, the early Gnostic heresy: 'The evil that is in the world must be due to the Creator of the world; it must be inherent in the world from the beginning — the result of some weakness at least, or some ignorance, if not of some positive malignity in its first formation.... The Redeemer of the world must stand higher than the Creator; for he is sent to remedy the imperfection of the Creator's work.' [1] Blake believed this thoroughly: 'Thinking as I do that the Creator of this world is a very cruel Being, and being a worshipper of Christ, I cannot help saying to the Son — Oh, how unlike the Father! First God Almighty comes with a thump on the head, and then Jesus Christ comes with a balm to heal it.'" [2]

Los, besides being time, is also the poet, the prophet of eternity in time. He keeps awake in man the memory of the land from whence he came. The entering of time into the fall is an act of mercy, thus bounds are given to error and the light of the poetical inspiration, which is the Spirit of God, the holy Ghost, shines in the darkness.

> "Los is by mortals nam'd Time, Enitharmon is named Space;
> But they depict him bald and agèd who is in eternal youth,
> All powerful, and his locks flourish like the brows of morning:
> He is the Spirit of Prophecy, the ever-apparent Elias.
> Time is the mercy of Eternity; without Time's swiftness,
> Which is the swiftest of all things, all were eternal torment" [3].

Los eternalises time and space:

> "not one Moment
> Of Time is lost, nor one Event of Space unpermanent;
> But all remain; every fabric of Six Thousand Years
> Remains permanent: tho, on the Earth, where Satan
> Fell and was cut off, all things vanish and are seen no more,
> They vanish not from me and mine; we guard them, first and last.
> The generations of men run on in the tide of Time,
> But leave their destin'd lineaments permanent for ever and ever [4].

---

[1] Mansel's *Gnostic Heresies*, Lect. II, quoted by Foster Damon, *William Blake, etc.*, p. 116.
[2] *M. S. Book*, quoted by Foster Damon, *William Blake, etc.*, p. 116.
[3] *Milton* I, 24, 68—74.
[4] *Ibid.*, 20, 18—26.

So in his bodily contraction man is not entirely deprived of the glory of eternity. In the poet's imagination it lives on, and in its light he lives his true life on earth.

The tragedy of the creation goes on and is enacted in different personages. Urizen is hit by Fuzon, one of his sons, who represents passion. The moment Fuzon with his globe of fire wounds his father, part of Urizen is separated from him, it is the sweet Ahania, the soul of pleasure, who henceforth is to be a faint shadow, moaning for her lost Urizen, circling round him as the moon does round the earth. The lament of Ahania for Urizen is a piece of beautiful poetry. It is a touching elegy of the forsaken heart, a cry of the woman for man, of man for God, the sobbing of the divided soul which yearns in its anguish for union with that which is its completion and fulfilment.

"Ah! Urizen! Love!
Flower of morning! I weep on the verge
Of Nonentity — how wide the abyss
Between Ahania and thee!

I lie on the verge of the deep,
I see thy dark clouds ascend;
I see thy black forests and floods,
A horrible waste to my eyes!

Weeping I walk over rocks,
Over dens, and thro' valleys of death.
Why did'st thou despise Ahania,
To cast me from thy bright presence
Into the World of Loneness?

I cannot touch his hand,
Nor weep on his knees, nor hear
His voice and bow, nor see his eyes
And joy; nor hear his footsteps, and
My heart leap at the lovely sound.
I cannot kiss the place
Whereon his bright feet have trod,
But I wander on the rocks
With hard necessity." [1]

---

[1] *Book of Ahania* V, 8—30.

Chapter VII

THE FOUR ZOAS. THE EMANATIONS

The figures of Urizen and Ahania, Los and Enitharmon, which I discussed in the preceding chapter, call for a further classification in the definite system in which Blake laid down his vision.

Man, who is a reflex of the universe, consists of four fundamental principles, which Blake calls the four Zoas and which we may trace back to the four beasts in Ezekiel's Vision and in the Apocalypse.[1] The "four mighty ones that are in every man" are Urizen, reason, intellect, Luvah, love, the emotions, Tharmas, the vegetative power and Urthona, the primal instinct, the universal spirit, which binds man to the world and God,[2] spiritual energy.[3] We can only make an attempt at defining them, for

"What are the Natures of those Living Creatures the Heavenly Father only Knoweth: No Individual Knoweth, nor Can Know in all Eternity."[4]

They have each a place in the universe, Urthona the North, Luvah the East, Urizen the South and Tharmas the West. When the Zoas keep their separate places, harmony lives in the world and in the human soul, but as soon as they leave their destined places, and invade another's dominion, harmonious quiet is disturbed.

One of the other fundamental characteristics of Blake's symbolism is the divisions of the Zoas and other spirits into spectre and emanation. The dualistic principle in the created universe is expressed by this. The emanation is man's imaginative faculty, his emotional capacity, which is mostly represented as a female, whilst the part that remains when the emanation has separated itself is the reasoning power, unemotional intellectualism, Pha-

[1] See Sloss and Wallis II, pp. 256, 257.
[2] See Berger, *William Blake, etc.*, p. 145.
[3] See Sloss and Wallis II, p. 193.
[4] *The four Zoas* I, 1, 7—9.

4

risaical self-righteousness, symbolized as a male, the spectre.

> "it is the Reasoning power,
> An Abstract, objecting power that Negatives everything.
> This is the Spectre of Man, the Holy Reasoning Power,
> And in its Holiness is closed the Abomination of Desolation." [1]

Los says of his spectre:

> "Thou art my Pride and my Self-righteousness; I have found thee out." [2]

Often a being only consists of spectre and emanation, but sometimes a third part remains after division, a kind of astral body, a shadow of former existence. The body of the Universal Man after his fall lying asleep on the Rock of Ages, is such a shadow. It also occurs that an individual remains essentially the same, and sees its spectre and emanation outside itself as hostile and friendly powers. Los is an example of such an individual.

Both spectre and emanation feel unhappy in their divided state and crave for union, as I observed, when I spoke about Ahania's lament for Urizen. Urthona is the only Zoa who does not appear divided, in the capacity of Universal Spirit, but he is manifested in a lower form as Los, whose emanation, as we saw in the preceding chapter, is Enitharmon. In the cosmic world Enitharmon is space, in the spiritual world she is spiritual beauty, which Los, the poet, yearns after. She is also the sensibility in the soul of the artist, his joy in his work, his emotion at his visions. [3] Luvah's emanation is Vala, who stands for natural beauty. To Tharmas, the body, the senses, belongs Enion, the generative instinct. The division of spectre and emanation, the fighting of the Zoas for each other's dominion, is the further fall from eternity, which had its beginning in Urizen's separation. The longest of Blake's poems, *Vala* or *The four Zoas*, describes this struggle of the Zoas and their final union in the universal Man, in the Divine. "For we wrestle not against flesh and blood, but against principalities, against powers, against the rulers of the darkness of this world, against spiritual wickedness in the high places." At the head of the first night [4] Blake put this quotation from *Ephesians*, as

[1] *Jerusalem* I, 10, 13—17.
[2] *Ibid.* 8, 30.
[3] See Berger, *William Blake, etc.*, pp. 179, 182.
[4] The poem is divided into nine parts, called "nights".

being the spiritual essence of the first part of his epic, whilst a marginal note by the side of line six, from *St. John*, expresses the mystic's yearning for unity and his inner vision of ultimate triumph. "That they all may be one, as thou, Father, art in me, and I in thee, that they also may be one in us: that the world may believe that thou hast sent me. And the glory which thou gavest me I have given them; that they may be one, even as we are one: I in them, and thou in me, that they may be made perfect in one, and that the world may know that thou hast sent me, and hast loved them as thou hast loved me."

We saw that the originator of the fall, the creation, was Urizen. In *the four Zoas* he is described as trying to usurp the kingdom of Urthona. We saw that his emanation, Ahania, was separated from him. "She represents the affective and emotional self in man, the 'soul of sweet delight', appetite, desire or lust. She is called sin by the restrictive powers in life, symbolized by Urizen." [1]

When Urizen gave his "horses of light" to Luvah, to be driven by the latter trough his dominion in the South and he fled to the North, the kingdom of Urthona, the unity in the Zoas was broken, the world began to shake on its foundations, man was wounded in the tenderest and most precious of his feelings, love began to suffer. Luvah fell, but Christ put on, in His loving mercy, Luvah's "robes of blood", and by incarnating Himself in this way, became the Saviour of fallen man.

Tharmas, the vegetative power, the body and the senses, resembles the shepherd of the *Songs of Innocence*, he who untroubled strays from morn till eve, guarding his flock. [2] Without Enion he is a despairing figure, wandering in search of his emanation. "He appears to represent Desire or Aspiration almost completely unimaginative." [3]

The aforegoing is only a short exposition of the framework on which Blake wove his visionary poetry. I shall not enter into all the obscure intricacies of the struggles of the Zoas, into their mutual relations, their dark genealogies. It would be a task belonging more to the sphere of psychology than of pure

---

[1] Sloss and Wallis II, p. 127.
[2] See Berger, *William Blake, etc.*, p. 151.
[3] Sloss and Wallis II, p. 236.

mysticism. It might besides prove an almost impossible and fruitless endeavour, and certainly it is not necessary for the purpose which I have set myself in writing this essay, the tracing of the e s s e n t i a l mystical element in both the works of Blake and Wordsworth, and a subsequent comparing of the two. [1]

---

[1] See for a further explanation of *The Zoas* Ellis and Yeats, Berger, *William Blake, etc.*, Foster Damon, *William Blake, etc.*, Sloss and Wallis.

Chapter VIII

THE REDEMPTION

Though with some reserve, I have ranked Blake among the religious mystics, because Christ is to him the Saviour of fallen man.[1] Man is symbolised by him in the symbol of Albion. He took Albion as the representative of humanity, because he believed that "Britain was the primitive seat of patriarchal religion."[2] All things begin and end in Albion's Ancient Druid Rocky Shore."[3] Albion is now lying in the sleep of death on "the rock of ages." "Eternity groan'd and was troubled at the image of eternal Death."[4] But the vision of God, which is "always present to the wise," the pleasure of God, which "unsought falls round the infant's path," it will again shine, with renewed brightness, after the purging flames of the jugdment-day, when all errors shall be annihilated.

And man, shrunk up into the limits of mortality, is still "translucent all within."

> "The Divine Vision still was seen,
> Still was the Human Form Divine,
> Keeping in weak and mortal Clay,
> O Jesus, still the Form was thine!"[5]

Blake believed in an immanent Divinity, both in man and in nature. The former seems to have appealed strongest to him.

---

[1] See Evelyn Underhill, *Mysticism*, p. 562.
[2] *Jerusalem, To the Jews*.
[3] *Ibid*. II, 32, 15.
"According to British mythology, Joseph of Arimathea brought the Holy Grail to Glastonbury, and there founded Christianity." (Foster Damon, *William Blake, etc.*, p. 447.)
[4] *The four Zoas* II, 10, 57.
[5] *Jerusalem, To the Jews*, 57—61.

> "the Worship of God is honouring His gifts
> In other men, and loving the greatest men best, each according
> To his Genius, which is the Holy Ghost in Man: there is no other
> God than that God who is the intellectual fountain of Humanity." [1]

This God in man is the imagination, which breaks through bodily opacity into the light of the spiritual world.

It is the "divine body of the Lord," [2] the eternal body of man, God Himself, the Divine body, Jesus, we are His members." [3] So God and Jesus are identified, because in Jesus Blake found the imagination preserved in its pristine and flaming vitality. He who was in the sanctuary of its hot blaze, lived life in its unsullied essence, in its deep emotionality. He found himself in God and God in Him. "I and the Father are one," Christ said. One of Blake's aphorisms written round an engraving of the Laocoön is "God is Jesus." From the foregoing it follows that by the word imagination Blake meant more than the faculty to raise mental images of things not present to the senses. With him it is the highest instinct in man, his infinite desire, in which he grasps the infinite, his boundless expansive power, which makes him "murmur in the flowers small as the honeybee" or "stretch across the heavens and step from star to star," [4] the transfusing flame, in whose glow all things shine forth in elemental splendour, which is love, ecstacy, mercy, beauty, truth, the mirror which reflects eternity's light.

Aglow with the emotion of heavenly vision Blake wanted to make his fellow-men, immersed in the sea of doubt and materialism, share the ecstacy of his bliss.

> "Trembling I sit day and night; my friends are astonish'd at me;
> Yet they forgive my wanderings. I rest not from my great task,
> To open the Eternal Worlds, to open the immortal Eyes
> Of Man inwards into the Worlds of Thought, into Eternity
> Ever expanding in the Bosom of God, the Human Imagination."

---

[1] *Jerusalem* IV, 91, 7—11.
See quotation 2 from *The Marriage of Heaven and Hell*, p. 41.
[2] *Jerusalem* I, 5, 59.
[3] Engraving of the *Laocoön*.
[4] *The four Zoas* II, 12, 505—507.
[5] *Jerusalem* I, 5, 15—21.

THE REDEMPTION

As I observed, in Christ the imagination flamed supreme. He only acted by the light of its revelation. His life was purely emotional and instinctive. He was "all virtue and acted from impulse, not from rules."[1] So Jesus is the supreme poet, the romanticist. He is the fierce opponent of the moralist, who prescribes outward rules for the spontaneous growth of inward life, of the experimentalist, who teaches doubt, instead of faith. He is the great individualist, to whom personality is the unimpeachable sanctuary of the spirit. "One Law for the Lion and Ox is Oppression."[2] "The apple tree never asks the beech how he shall grow; nor the lion the horse how he shall take his prey."[3] Los, the poet, stands over against Urizen, the stern law-giver, who is often identified by Blake with the God of the Old Testament, who gave to Moses on Mount Sinai his ten commandments, which were broken by Christ, "who mocked at the sabbath, and so mocked the sabbath's God; murdered those who were murdered because of Him; turned away the law from the woman taken in adultery, stole the labour of others to support Him, bore false witness, when He omitted making a defence before Pilate; coveted when he prayed for his disciples, and when he bid them shake off the dust of their feet against such as refused to lodge him."[4] In these debatable paradoxes Blake tried to sanctify the liberty of the imagination. In *The everlasting Gospel* he laid down an important part of his conception of Christ. He is aware of the gulf of difference which separates his vision of the Saviour from the traditional one.

> "The Vision of Christ that thou dost see
> Is my vision's greatest enemy.
> Thine has a great hook-nose like thine;
> Mine has a snub-nose like to mine.
> Thine is the Friend of all Mankind;
> Mine speaks in parables to the blind."[5]

The Christ with "the hook-nose" is the humble, the gentle, the meek, he with "the snub-nose" is the passionate rebel, who

---

[1] *The Marriage of Heaven and Hell, A Memorable Fancy.*
[2] *Ibid., A Memorable Fancy.*
[3] *Ibid., Proverbs of Hell.*
[4] *Ibid., A Memorable Fancy.*
[5] *The everlasting Gospel,* 1—7.

with unparalleled vigour fights sham-religion, sham-morality, anything false, anything that obstructs the free stream of life. Blake does not look upon Him as the Son of the immaculate Virgin. His Mother was purely human, just as He was Himself, subject to human passions, and in being purely human He was most purely divine. Mary Magdalene is taken up by Him in the bosom of His all-comprising feeling of life, which also encloses among its boundless treasures the precious gem of the forgiveness of sins. He does not condemn her, but his indignation goes out in burning fierceness against those who by restraining life's true energies pollute its purity, desecrate its sanctity and commit the one deadly sin of the Pharisee, who thanks his God in self-righteous conceit, that he is not as his fellow-sinner. Christ is put over against Bacon and Newton, the types for Blake of the mere intellect. Their belief is that

> "God can only be known by his attributes.
> And as to the indwelling of the Holy Ghost,
> Or of Christ and the Father, it's all a boast
> And pride and vanity of imagination,
> That disdains to follow this world's fashion." [1]

Foster Damon thinks the epigrammatic brilliancy of *The everlasting Gospel* shocking, nearly to the point of blasphemy. But the spirit behind it is not blasphemy, he says. "It was the fierce bitterness of his attack on the false god worshipped under the divine name, and a confidence of familiarity with his own deity that made Blake write as he did." [2]

There is beauty in the stormy passion, the lightening vehemence with which hypocrisy and dead formalism are denounced. The tenderness of forgiving love is enshrined in it, but yet we are shown only the negative side of the great affirmation which was Christ. "Think not that I am come to destroy the law or the prophets. I am not come to destroy, but to fulfil," He said. The fulfilment brought destruction in its wake, but the destruction was lost in the consummation of the fulfilment. In *The everlasting Gospel* it is almost the other way about.

---

[1] *The everlasting Gospel*, 44—49.
[2] Foster Damon, *William Blake, etc.*, p. 129.

> "If Thou humblest Hyself, Thou humblest Me.
> Thou also dwell'st in Eternity.
> Thou art a Man: God is no more:
> Thy own Humanity learn to adore," [1]

God says to Christ.

Swinburne, speaking of *The Marriage of Heaven and Hell*, in which Blake puts forth a similar conception of the Deity, says: "The very root and kernel of this creed is not the assumed humanity of God, but the achieved divinity of man." Of *The everlasting Gospel* he says: "There is more absolute worship implied in it than in most works of art that pass muster as religious, a more perfect power of noble adoration, an intenser faculty of faith and capacity of love, keen as flame and soft as light, a more uncontrollable desire for right and lust after justice, a more inexhaustible grace of pity for all evil and sorrow that is not of itself pitiless, a more deliberate sweetness of mercy towards all that are cast out and trodden under." [2]

Gardner in his *Vision and Vesture* is not so eulogistic as Swinburne. He gives as the immediate cause of the writing of *The everlasting Gospel* Blake's resentment against Stothard, who, according to him, had stolen his design for *The Canterbury Pilgrimage*. "Then he found excuse and encouragement for his anger and indignation in Christ, who was proud, wrathful, gentle to unchastity, disobedient. But as Blake studied this strange life deeper, his spirit kindled. Jesus always forgave sins. As Blake read and pondered, he rose above his excrementitious resentments and attained the Christ-level, where he could understand and forgive." [4]

> "God appears, and God is Light,
> To those poor souls that dwell in Night;
> But does a Human Form display
> To those that dwell in realms of Day." [5]

This is another of the many passages in which Blake avows

---

[1] *The everlasting Gospel*, 73—77.
[2] Swinburne, *William Blake*, p. 240.
[3] *Ibid.*, *William Blake*, p. 194.
[4] Gardner, *Vision and Vesture*, p. 40.
[5] *Auguries of Innocence*, 129—132.

his belief in a personal-human Deity. Chesterton's opinion is that the last two lines express all that is best in Blake and all that is best in all the tradition of the mystics.[1] Personally I think that the truth of this statement may be called in question, that this belief, so very strongly marked, is one of the reasons why Blake's art, notwithstanding its great spirituality, often makes an opposite impression, that instead of "spiritualizing the natural, he is apt to naturalize the spiritual."[2]

It is one of the fundamental characteristics of his philosophy, which also finds expression in his "outline-theory," in his predilection for the Florentine- to the Venetian and Dutch School in art. "The great and golden rule of art, as well as of life, is this: that the more distinct, sharp and wiry the bounding line, the more perfect the work of art; and the less keen and sharp the greater is the evidence of weak imitation, plagiarism and bungling."[3]

Most probably in his vision of a personal-human God he underwent the influence of Swedenborg, who said in his *Angelic Wisdom concerning divine Love*: "God is very man. In all heavens there is no other idea of God than the idea of a man. To think of holiness distinct from man, is impossible to the affection."[4] One of the resolutions passed by the first Conference of the Swedenborg Society on Easter-Monday, 1789, signed by Blake and Catherina, his wife, is that "all Faith and Worship directed to any other than the one God, Jesus Christ, in His Divine Humanity, being directed to a God invisible and in comprehensible, have a direct tendency to overturn the Holy Word and to destroy everything spiritual in the Church."[5] To Lavater's aphorism: "He who adores an impersonal God has none, and without guide or rudder launches on an immense abyss that first absorbs his powers, and next himself," Blake makes the annotation : "Most superlative beautiful, and most affectionately holy and pure. Would to God

---

[1] Chesterton, *William Blake*, p. 147.
[2] Wilkinson, *Preface to the Songs of Innocence and Experience*.
[3] Quoted from Basil de Selincourt, *William Blake*, p. 130.
[4] Quoted by Ellis in *The Real Blake*, p. 33.
[5] H. N. Morris, *Blake and Swedenborg, the Quest* XI, Oct. 1919.

THE REDEMPTION

that all men would consider it."[1] It is difficult to gather from Blake's writings, a definite conception of God and Christ."[2] When we read the resolution of the Swedenborg Conference we are inclined to think that the personal God in whom he believes is Christ, when we read the annotation to Lavater's aphorisms we might think that God and Christ are not identified. When we read "God only Acts and Is in existing beings or Men,"[3] we cannot gather anything from it but a belief in God as man's highest spiritual powers, but in "God is man and exists in us and we in him,"[4] the deification of man is weakened by a very slight difference. Crabb Robinson reports of Blake: "On my asking in what light he viewed the great question concerning the Divinity of Jesus Christ, he said: 'He is the only God.' But then he added .... 'And so am I and so are you.'[5] In the Ghost of Abel Christ, the Saviour, and God, the Creator, are identified. Satan says to Jehovah: "Thou shalt Thyself be sacrificed to Me, thy God, on Calvary." In Crabb Robinson's diary we further read: "'Christ was wrong in suffering Himself to be crucified, He should not have attacked the Government. He had no business with such matters.' On my inquiring how he reconciled this with the sanctity and divine qualities of Jesus, he said, He was not then become the Father. Connecting as well as one can these fragmentary sentiments, it would be hard to give Blake's station between Christianity, Platonism and Spinozism. Yet he professes to be very hostile to Plato and reproaches Wordsworth with being not a Christian but a Platonist."[6] If Blake meant what he said (and the question suggests itself to me, whether he did not speak on purpose in a provokingly ambiguous and puzzling way), he showed a serious lack of insight into Christ's character. In *Milton* his belief seems far from being so heretical, when he testifies to his veneration for the Methodist preachers,

---

[1] Quoted by Ellis in *The real Blake*, p. 65.
[2] See Ellis and Yeats II, p. 250.
[3] *The Marriage of Heaven and Hell*, A Memorable Fancy.
[4] *Marginalia* to Berkeley's *Siris*.
[5] Crabb Robinson, *Diary*, 10 Dec., 1825.
[6] *Ibid.*

Whitefield and Wesley, who in the midst of all kinds of unbelief called for:

> "Faith in God the dear Saviour, who took on the likeness of men,
> Becoming obedient to death, even the death of the Cross." [1]

To Hayley he wrote in 1805: "The mocker of art is the mocker of Jesus. Let us go on, dear Sir, following his Cross."

Gilchrist wrote: "In society people would disbelieve and exasperate him, would set upon the gentle, fiery-hearted mystic, and stir him up into being extravagant out of a mere spirit of opposition. Then he would say things on purpose to startle and make people stare. In the excitement of conversation he would exaggerate his peculiarities of opinion and doctrine, would express a floating vision or fancy in an extreme way, without the explanation or qualification he was, in reality, well aware it needed; taking a secret pleasure in the surprise and opposition such views aroused."[2]

Towards the conclusion of his study on Blake Story observes: "No one, perhaps, can have read thus far in Blake without perceiving that he cannot always be taken 'au pied de la lettre,' in other words, that there is sometimes a touch of perversity in what he says, and that he takes especial delight in a bold paradox."[3]

I shall quote some more of Crabb Robinson's conversation with him. Perhaps it throws additional light on the question how far we can take Blake at his word with respect to this. It abounds in strange, confusing, contradictory conceptions, puzzling, irritating obscurities and heresies.

"'There is no use in education. I hold it wrong. It is the great sin. It is eating of the tree of knowledge of good and evil. That was the fault of Plato. He knew of nothing but of the virtues and vices and good and evil. There is nothing in all that. Everything is good in God's eyes.' On my putting the question: 'Is there

---

[1] *Milton* I, 20, 57—59.
[2] Gilchrist, *The Life of William Blake*, ch. XXXV, quoted by Foster Damon, *William Blake, etc.*, p. 198. See note: "Every one of Blake's friends confirms this. See f. e. Tatham's *Life* (pp. 38—39); Linnell's letter to Bernard Barton (*Letters of William Blake*, p. 229) and Palmer's Letter quoted by Gilchrist, ch. XXXIII."
[3] Story, *William Blake, etc.*, p. 144.

nothing absolutely evil in what men do?' 'I am no judge of that. Perhaps not in God's eyes.' Yet at other times he spoke of error as being in Heaven. I asked about the moral character of Dante in writing his vision. 'Was he pure?' 'Do you think there is any purity in God's eye?' "

But whatever may be the exact meaning of Blake's obscure statements, however expansive his conception of God and Christ may be, however much it may fluctuate according to the moods of his capricious, whimsical mind, it is certain that to him the imagination is godlike, as I observed on page 54; that, according to him, by means of it man enters into the Kingdom of God, or rather is that Kingdom itself. "I know of no other Christianity and of no other Gospel than the liberty both of body and mind to exercise the Divine Arts of Imagination. Imagination, the real and Eternal World of which this Vegetable Universe is but a faint shadow and in which we shall live in our Eternal or Imaginative Bodies, when these Vegetable Mortal Bodies are no more. The Apostles knew of no other Gospel." [1] I have also drawn attention to the fact that to Blake Jesus was the supreme poet. In Him religion and art were fused into one harmonious unity. He who pierced with his sparkling imagination into the minutest particle of spirit and thus lived in His great soul the universal life, He made his pilgrimage on earth a song of the rarest melody, a work of art transcending all others.

The following aphorisms from *The Laocoön* all express this belief in the divinity of art.

"Jesus and His Apostles and Disciples were all Artists. Their Works were destroy'd by the Seven Angels of the Seven Churches in Asia, Antichrist, Science.
The Old and New Testaments are the great codes of Art.
The whole Business of Man Is The Arts, and All Things Common.
Art is the Tree of Life.
A Poet, a Painter, a Musician, an Architect — the Man Or Woman who is not one of these is not a Christian.
Art Degraded, Imagination Denied, War Governed the Nations."

Gardner in his *Vision and Vesture* especially treats Blake in the light of this conception of art and Christianity being identical.

[1] *Jerusalem, To the Christians.*

"Blake's glory and Blake's significance to our age is just this, that religion and art were passionately fused in his own soul, and it is only by doing full justice to both, and by presenting him and his message whole and undivided, that one can hope to write worthily of a genius at once the most creative and the most religious produced by the western world." [1] De Selincourt expresses himself in a similar spirit. "Gilchrist maintains that his identification of art with Christianity meant no more than that the idea pleased him and that in consequence 'his heart told him that it was true.' [2] Very few of Blake's ideas have, in fact, any other sanction. He thought what it pleased him to think. But his idea of Christianity as Art is one of the most fundamental and one of the most explicit of his ideas. And there is none that rouses him to a greater passion of feeling. Indeed we are touching here not upon his theory but upon himself. Art was his one activity, and with him it was a religious activity in the fullest sense of the word: 'The whole of the New Church is in the active life.' He could not in himself distinguish his religion from his art: 'I know of no other Christianity, and of no other Gospel, than the liberty both of body and mind to exercise the divine Arts of Imagination.' Perhaps it is his highest and noblest achievement, to have maintained in his life a genuine fusion of the two." [3]

Before finishing this discussion of Blake's conception of Christ, I wish to draw attention to the fact that Oscar Wilde in his *De Profundis* has a kindred vision of Him. In the above-mentioned book he says that the basis of His nature was a flamelike imagination and that thus His place is among the poets, and that only by the imagination, the poetical instinct, He can be truly understood. Like the Christ of Blake's *The everlasting Gospel* He is a lover of sinners and a hater of the hypocritically righteous. [4]

What I have said about Blake's conception of Christ applies to a great extent to Him as He lived His life on earth as a human

---

[1] Gardner, *Vision and Vesture*, p. 10.
[2] Crabb Robinson, *Diary*, 10 Dec. 1825.
[3] De Selincourt, *William Blake*, p. 147.
[4] See Kassner, *Die Mystik, die Künstler und das Leben*, p. 374, Von Taube, *Die Ethik der Fruchtbarkeit*, p. 36, Gardner, *Vision and Vesture*, p. 177, Foster Damon, *William Blake, etc.*, p. 249.

being. In Blake we also find a vision of Him, which I have already touched upon, as the symbol of the Spirit which eternally gives itself to man and thus saves him from eternal death; he rises above him, and is seen by Blake hovering over him, while writing Jerusalem in the illumination of poetical inspiration, calling upon Albion to awake from death into life eternal.

"Of the Sleep of Ulro;[1] and of the passage through
Eternal Death, and of the awakening to Eternal Life.
This theme calls me in sleep night after night and ev'ry morn
Awakes me at sun-rise; then I see the Saviour over me
Spreading his beams of love, and dictating the words of this mild song."[2]

But this Saviour, who rises above man, mystically descends to the level of him and speaks the gospel-words:

"I am not a God afar off: I am a brother and a friend;
Within your bosoms I reside, and you reside in me.
Lo! we are one! forgiving all Evil, Not Seeking recompense."[3]

Albion is still asleep, still in a divided state, still dominated by the evil influence of his spectre. When his emanation Jerusalem, the symbol of liberty, shall be united to him, the spectre shall exist no longer and the union of man and God shall be achieved, the truth of Christ's words:

"I am not a God afar off, I am a brother and a friend,
Within your bosoms I reside and you reside in me,"

shall be fully lived.

"Each man is in his spectre's power
Until the arrival of that hour
When his humanity awake
And cast his spectre into the lake."[4]

Listen to Blake's fervent prayer to Christ, the Lamb of God:

[1] Ulro is the world of matter.
[2] *Jerusalem* I, 4, 1—4.
[3] *Ibid.*, 4, 16—18.
[4] *Ibid.*, 41.

> "Come to my arms and never more
> Depart, but dwell for ever here;
> Create my Spirit to thy Love;
> Subdue my Spectre to thy Fear." [1]

Christ and Los may often be identified to a certain extent, and this will be quite clear, when we consider that Los is the symbolic representation of the prophetic spirit, that part in man which is able to communicate with the world of undivided spirits, in which he lived before the creation. Christ is the symbol of the absolute spirit, which is beyond division, Los is the symbol of the spirit as it lives in man and has to fight against the power of its spectre. Los fights his spectre, who hovers over him as a blackening shadow, with indomitable courage. He is victorious and even compels his enemy to work with him for the benefit of Albion. In *Jerusalem* he is represented as a blacksmith, labouring at his huge furnaces and forging on his anvil of iron.

"The blow of his Hammer is Justice, the swing of his Hammer Mercy:
The force of Los's Hammer is eternal Forgiveness." [2]

The sons and daughters of Albion, who represent the evil, selfish qualities in man, are thrown into the purifying flames of Los's furnaces, out of which they rise, regenerated, instinct with Los's spirit, becoming Los's assistants in his building of the great city of art, Golgonooza, [3] the huge work of inspiration, which shines in the history of humanity. *The four Zoas* contains only a little of the construction of this world of art; the greater part of it is described in *Jerusalem*. Blake gives us a very minute description of it. It is reminiscent of Ezekiel's vision of the four-fold temple with its many divisions and details, of St. John's four-fold city. This division into four corresponds with the four Zoas. All that has stirred the human soul from the time of its incarnation on earth, all that has been performed by man exists in the city of art.

> "All things acted on Earth are seen in the bright Sculptures of
> Los's Halls, and every Age renews its powers from these Works,

---

[1] *Jerusalem* II, *To the Jews*.
[2] *Ibid.*, II, 88, 49—51.
[3] "The root of the word seems to be 'Golgotha', since all Art is self-sacrifice." (Foster Damon, *William Blake, etc.*, p. 375.)

THE REDEMPTION

With every pathetic story possible to happen from Hate or
Wayward Love; and every sorrow and distress is carved here;
Every Affinity of Parents, Marriages, and Friendships are here
In all their various combinations, wrought with wondrous Art,
All that can happen to Man in his pilgrimage of seventy years." [1]

Foster Damon says of it: "This celebrated passage means more than that everything is contained in Art, or in Eternity. Blake is retelling quite clearly one of the most persistent of all occult theories. This is the theory of the 'Cosmic Memory,' in which all images and events of the Past and the Future are preserved. Soothsayers and clairvoyants claim to penetrate this Memory; and by beholding those Ideas which are descending to birth on the material plane, they can foretell the future. This theory is to be found in Indian, Greek, Egyptian, Celtic and Jewish thought. It is the 'Perfect Land' of the Egyptian mysteries, it is Plato's World of Ideas, it is the 'Yesod '(Archetypal World), of the Kabalah, the 'Astral Plane' (or Light) of later Occultists and the 'Akashic Records' of Theosophy." [2] Thus Blake, besides being considered as a mystic is also given a place among the occultists. But whatever may be the exact meaning Blake put into the abovementioned quotation, to me, who treats Blake as a mystic, preeminently as a mystic poet, the idea of everything being contained in art, in eternity, is the most important. It is the great, purely spiritual thought, which occurs again and again in Blake's poetry. In essence it is the same truth that is so beautifully expressed in the lines which speak of the boundless love of the Saviour:

"he suffers with those that suffer.
For not one sparrow can suffer, and the whole Universe not suffer also
In all its Regions, and its Father and Saviour not pity and weep!" [3]

We have it in the *Auguries of Innocence*:

"A robin redbreast in a cage
Puts all Heaven in a rage.
A dove-house fill'd with doves and pigeons
Shudders Hell thro' all its regions."

[1] *Jerusalem* I, 16, 61—68.
[2] Foster Damon, *William Blake, etc.*, p. 443.
See Evelyn Underhill, *Mysticism*, p. 186.
[3] *Jerusalem* I, 25, 7—10.

It is also at the root of its highly imaginative opening lines:

> "To see a World in a grain of sand,
> And a Heaven in a wild flower,
> Hold infinity in the palm of your hand,
> And Eternity in an hour."

It is Los, the poet, who eternalizes time and space.

> "not one Moment
> Of Time is lost, nor one Event of Space unpermanent;
> But all remain; every fabric of Six Thousand Years
> Remains permanent: tho' on the Earth, where Satan
> Fell and was cut off, all things vanish and are seen no more,
> They vanish not from me and mine; we guard them, first and last.
> The generations of men run on in the tide of Time,
> But leave their destin'd lineaments permanent for ever and ever."[1]

It is the A.B.C. of mysticism, the beholding of the undivided Light through and in the brokenness of appearances, the eternalizing of life's fleeting actions and moments in the fixed ground of things, the vision of the one in the multitude and of the multitude in the One, who by Blake is seen as Man, the divine man, the human God, Christ, who includes everything, also the city of Golgonooza,

> "for, contracting our infinite senses,
> We behold multitude; or, expanding, we behold as one,
> As One Man, all the Universal Family; and that One Man
> We call Jesus the Christ: and he in us, and we in him
> Live in perfect harmony in Eden, the land of life,
> Giving, recieving, and forgiving each others' trespasses.
> He is the Good shepherd, he is the Lord and master;
> He is the Shepherd of Albion, he is all in all
> In Eden, in the garden of God, and in heavenly Jerusalem."[2]

As Blake advanced in life the mystery of Christ's forgiving of sins penetrated deeper into his consciousness. Its gleam shines through the whole of Jerusalem. It is Blake's firm belief that not before Christ is reborn so entirely in the heart of man, that the latter lives in the completeness of the spirit of forgiving with

---

[1] *Milton* I, 20, 18—26.
[2] *Jerusalem* II, 38, 17—26.

respect to his fellow-creatures, shall he be saved. With St. Paul Blake admonishes us: "Forbear one another, forgive one another, if any man have a quarrel against any: even as Christ forgave you, so also do ye." [1] With St. Paul he knew redemption to exist in the inflow of Christ's spirit into the heart. "I am crucified with Christ: nevertheless I live; yet not I, but Christ liveth in me."[2] So his mystic feeling had grown into something which dived deeper into the mystery of the Christian salvation than the spirit which created *The Marriage of Heaven and Hell*. We have seen what Blake said about the doctrine of the atonement to Crabb Robinson.

A third aspect of Blake's vision of Christ, which we may call the cosmic one, remains to be discussed. I mentioned Blake's belief that the creation was an act of mercy, notwithstanding its depriving man of his greatest bliss. There is a limit of opaqueness, it is called Satan, it is impossible for any creature to be more darkened in spirit than he, there is also a limit of contraction, it is Adam. Between him and Eternity stretches the longest distance possible that can separate man from God. The Saviour's act of mercy consists in forming a woman from the limit of contraction, so from Adam, that He Himself may in process of time be born of her in order to redeem man. Blake pierces into the inner life of eternity, where he sees the light of redeeming mercy in the incarnation of the Lamb of God shine even before the formation of the world:

> "we now behold
> Where Death Eternal is put off Eternally.
> Assume the dark Satanic body in the Virgin's womb,
> O Lamb divine! it cannot thee annoy! O pitying one!
> Thy pity is from the foundation of the World and thy Redemption
> Begun already in Eternity." [3]

Evelyn Underhill says with regard to this passage that it is curious to notice that the more inspired Blake's utterance, the more passionately and dogmatically Christian even this hater

---

[1] *Colossians* III, 13.
[2] *Galatians* II, 20.
[3] *The four Zoas* VIII, 6, 230—235.

of the Churches becomes. It is the doctrine of the Incarnation in a nutshell: here St. Thomas himself would find little to correct. [1]

Christ, Satan, Adam, are the great cosmic figures who symbolically represent the fundamental mystic truths by which the world lives. According to the doctrine of correspondences which sets forth the external and inward, the bodily and spiritual similarity of things, they also live in each individual man. Therefore it is possible that

> "there is no Limit of Expansion; there is no Limit of Translucence
> In the bosom of Man for ever from eternity to eternity," [2]

that man, even in his earthly life, while the opacity of his body encloses him, can enjoy the vision of God. And this happens in the mystic's trance, the poet's ecstacy, the prophet's dream, when the understanding is "in the spiritual light" [3] and the "sensations of the body are laid asleep." [3] Thus we come again to the immanent Christ, the Saviour "who is not a God afar off," but who "resides in us and we in Him," the Christ whom St. Paul felt living in the death of his crucifixion.

I have treated the different aspects of Jesus separately, but we must not forget that together they constitute Blake's one great vision of the Redeemer. They are not to be separated in essence, the one includes the other, they are united in mystic correlation. Blake's vision of the Redeemer is his vision of life itself. It is quite natural that he who beheld "a world in a grain of sand, a heaven in a wild flower," who saw all earthly things shining in the bright sculptures of the eternal city of art, who felt the suffering of one little sparrow spread through the whole universe, should see the Saviour as he did, outside space, in the unsearchable depths of eternity, and immanent, descending to the meanest creature that lives by the inspiration of His mercy. In this vision of Blake we can trace again affinity with Swedenborg, who says in *Angelic Wisdom concerning divine Love*: "The

---

[1] Evelyn Underhill, *Mysticism*, 127.
[2] *Jerusalem* II, 42, 35—37.
[3] Swedenborg, *Angelic Wisdom concerning divine Love*.

Divine in the whole heaven and the Divine in an angel is the same, wherefore the whole heaven can appear as one angel — The church, an entire society of Heaven, has appeared as one man, — as big as a giant — as small as an infant. The Divine is the same in greatest things and least things."

As I observed on page 66, the great divine message which Christ according to Blake, brought to the world was the forgiveness of sins. Even in *The everlasting Gospel* Blake proclaimed this belief. In the additional lines to this poem, which are only published in Keynes's edition, he expresses himself very definitely about it.

"There is not one Moral Virtue that Jesus Inculcated but Plato and Cicero did Inculcate before him; what then did Christ Inculcate? Forgiveness of Sins. This alone is the Gospel and this is the Life and Immortality brought to Light by Jesus. Even the Covenant of Jehovah which is This: 'If you forgive one another your Trespasses, so shall Jehovah forgive you, That he himself may dwell among you; but if you Avenge, you murder the Divine Image, and he cannot dwell among you; because you murder him he arises again, and you deny that he is arisen, and are blind to Spirit.' " [1] He repeats the same thought in the second stanza of these additional lines:

> "What can this Gospel of Jesus be?
> What Life and Immortality?
> What was it that he brought to Light,
> That Plato and Cicero did not write?
> The Heathen Deities wrote them all,
> These moral Virtues, great and small.
> What is the Accusation of Sin
> But Moral Virtues' deadly Gin?
> The Moral Virtues in their Pride
> Did o'er the World triumphant ride
> In Wars and Sacrifice for Sin,
> And Souls to Hell ran trooping in.
> The Accuser, Holy God of All,
> This Pharisaic Worldly Ball,
> Amidst them in his Glory Beams
> Upon the Rivers and the Streams.
> Then Jesus rose and said to Me:
> 'Thy Sins are all forgiven thee.'

---

[1] *Preface to The everlasting Gospel.*

> Loud Pilate Howled, loud Caiphas yelled,
> When they the Gospel Light beheld.
> It was when Jesus said to Me,
> 'Thy Sins are all forgiven thee.'
> The Christian trumpets loud proclaim
> Thro' all the World in Jesus' name
> Mutual forgiveness of each Vice,
> And oped the Gates of Paradise.
> The Moral Virtues in Great fear
> Formed the Cross and Nails and Spear,
> And the Accuser standing by,
> Cried out: 'Crucify! Crucify!' "

The proclamation of this truth is repeated again and again. To Albion's question, whether man cannot exist without mysterious offering of self for another, Jesus answered:

> "Wouldest thou love one who never died
> For thee, or ever die for one who had not died for thee?
> And if God dieth not for Man and giveth not himself
> Eternally for Man, Man could not exist; for Man is Love,
> As God is Love." [1]

The fervent hymn of the Virgin is an exultant glorification of the forgiveness of sins as the central point of mystic Christianity:

> "if I were pure, never could I taste the sweets
> Of the Forgiveness of Sins; if I were holy, I never could behold the tears
> Of love." [2]

> "O Mercy! O Divine Humanity!
> O Forgiveness and Pity and Compassion! If I were Pure I should never
> Have known Thee. If I were Unpolluted I should never have
> Glorified thy Holiness, or rejoiced in thy great Salvation." [3]

Evelyn Underhill says of the first quotation from *Jerusalem* that it is an almost perfect epitome of Christian theology and ethics; of the second and third she remarks that it is but a poet's gloss on the Catholic's cry "O felix culpa!" She quotes these passages in connection with her statement that "the Christian system or some colourable imitation of it, has been found essential by

---

[1] *Jerusalem* IV, 96, 23—28.
[2] *Ibid.* III, 61, 11—13.
[3] *Ibid.*, 43—47.

almost all the great mystics of the West," [1] even by Blake, especially in his inspired utterances, though he is a fierce hater of the Churches.

After having discussed at some length Blake's general view of the redemption, I shall give short extracts from the three *Prophetic Books* which deal with it: *Jerusalem, The four Zoas*, and *Milton*.

We saw that Albion lies bound on a rock, the rock of ages. He is asleep, as if in the sleep of death, because he has rejected his emanation, Jerusalem. The Saviour, spreading His beams of love over the poet, dictates the words of his mild song:

> "Awake! awake! O sleeper of the land of shadows, wake! expand!
> I am in you, and you in me, mutual in love divine,
> Fibres of love from man to man thro' Albion's pleasant land!
> In all the dark Atlantic vale down from the hills of Surrey
> A black water accumulates: return, Albion! return!
> Thy brethren call thee; and thy fathers and thy sons,
> Thy nurses and thy mothers, thy sisters and thy daughters
> Weep at thy soul's disease, and the Divine Vision is darken'd.
> Thy Emanation that was wont to play before thy face,
> Beaming forth with her daughters into the Divine bosom, —
> Where hast thou hidden thy Emanation, lovely Jerusalem,
> From the vision and fruition of the Holy-one?" [2]

Los sings of the splendour of Jerusalem, whom he sees shining in a luminous vision. He sees her as a six-winged seraph, richly coloured in azure, gold and purple, sparkling with the irridescence of immortal gems. Fiercely contrasted to this diaphanous loveliness is the description of the dead Albion, lying cold on a rock, storms and snows beating round him, roaring seas dashing furiously against him, whilst in the deep darkness which surrounds him, lightnings glare and thunders roll. The weeds of death enwrap his hands and feet, and over him the famished eagle screams on bony wings and around him howls the wolf of famine. But "the breath divine went over the morning hills." Albion awoke, and into the Heavens he walked, clothed in fire, speaking the words of Eternity. Then Jesus appeared to Albion in the similitude of

---

[1] Evelyn Underhill, *Mysticism*, p. 127.
[2] *Jerusalem* I, 4, 4—16.

Los, standing by him as the Good Shepherd, and He gathered His Sheep in the communion of the gospel of self-sacrifice and forgiveness of sins.

> "Self was lost in the contemplation of faith
> And wonder at the Divine Mercy and at Los's sublime honour." [1]

And Albion called his emanation from death into eternal day.

> "Awake, awake, Jerusalem: O lovely Emanation of Albion,
> Awake and overspread all Nations as in ancient Time.
> For lo! the Night of Death is past, and the Eternal Day
> Appears upon our hills. Awake, Jerusalem, and come away. [2]

The four Zoas appeared and shot their "intellectual arrows" through the wide Heavens. Man stood in his ancient four-fold glory. Humanity, revealed in all natural phenomena, was called to life again in the bosom of the Eternal:

"All Human Forms identified, even Tree, Metal, Earth, and Stone; all
Human Forms identified, living, going forth and returning wearied
Into the Planetary lives of Years, Months, Days and Hours; reposing,
And then Awaking into his Bosom in the Life of Immortality.
And I heard the Name of their Emanations: they are named Jerusalem." [3]

At the end of the book of *Jerusalem* Blake drew a picture of the soul in the embrace of God; it is the representation of the mystic's ultimate union. It is also treated in the other *Prophetic Books*, *The four Zoas* and *Milton*, though in a different form. I took *Jerusalem* as the frame in which Blake's vision of the redemption is enclosed, because it seems to me, notwithstanding its often hopeless obscurity of detail, the most simple in outline and most representative of the essential yearning and attainment of the mystic. According to Sampson it contains the completest statement of Blake's fully developed system of mythology. [4] Though it contains the names of countless mythical personages, whose exact place and function in Blake's scheme of the resurrection it is impossible to fix, yet the two figures of Albion and Jerusalem stand

---
[1] *Jerusalem* IV, 96, 31—33.
[2] *Ibid.*, 97, 1—5.
[3] *Ibid.*, 99, 57—61.
[4] Sampson, *Bibliographical Introduction to the Oxford Edition*.

out in definite outline, in so far as Blake's creations can ever be given the qualification of definiteness. Besides, it is most saturated with the spirit of Christian mysticism. In connection with the fact that Jerusalem was the last of his prophetic books it is important to notice that Christ, in whom Blake saw from beginning to end the Redeemer of the world, inspired him in Jerusalem to a fervour of prayer and adoration, to a depth of devotional mystic feeling that we do not find in *The four Zoas* and *Milton*.

In the former poem the redemption is seen as the union of the four Zoas with their respective emanations, and the awaking of the eternal man from the sleep of death on the Rock of Ages. We saw that the latter part of this vision is the chief subject of Jerusalem. In this poem it takes a subordinate place. The union of the four Zoas is described in the ninth night, called "the last Judgment." This last judgment consists in a throwing out of error, after which union can be actieved. "Whenever any individual rejects error and embraces truth, a Last Judgment passes upon that individual .... Error is created, truth is eternal. Error or creation will be burned up, and then, and not till then, "truth or eternity will appear." [1] According to the old doctrine of the macrocosm being repeated in the microcosm, the last judgment is universal and it is also achieved in each individual life.

Christ releases Los and Enitharmon from their bodies and the former destroys the visible universe, the world of error:

> "Los his vegetable hands
> Outstretch'd; his right hand, branching out in fibrous strength,
> Seiz'd the Sun; His left hand like dark roots, cover'd the Moon,
> And tore them down, cracking the heavens across from immense to
> immense." [2]

Then the fires of eternity fall, the heavens are shaken, the earth removed from its place, the trumpets thunderingly call the dead to judgment from the four winds. The thrones of kings fall, the oppressors are pursued by the oppressed, the wild beasts of the forests tremble:

> "the Lion shuddering asks the Leopard: Feelest thou
> The dread I feel, unknown before? My voice refuses to roar,

[1] *The Vision of the last Judgment.*
[2] *The four Zoas* IX, 1, 6—10.

And in weak moans I speak to thee. This night,
Before the morning's dawn, the Eagle call'd the Vulture,
The Raven call'd the hawk. I heard them from my forests,
Saying: 'Let us go up far, for soon I smell upon the wind
A terror coming from the south,' " [1]

The Eternal Man, Albion, begins to awake. Urizen gives up his authority over the four Zoas and appears in his ancient glory. He arose

"As on a Pyramid of mist, his white robes scattering
The fleecy white. Renew'd, he shook his agèd mantles off
Into the fires. Then glorious, bright, Exulting in his joy,
He sounding rose into the heavens in naked majesty,
In radiant Youth." [2]

Those who are accused while innocent shine with immortal glory, and the judge is seized with the terror of his guilt.

"trembling, the Judge springs from his throne,
Hiding his face in the dust beneath the prisoner's feet, and saying:
'Brother of Jesus, what have I done? Intreat thy Lord for me!
Perhaps I may be forgiven!' " [3]

Then all the nations see the vision of God. Blake, who in this poem is very strongly influenced by the Revelation of St. John describes Him as coming upon a cloud sitting on a throne, surrounded by twenty-four patriarchs, and these again surrounded by four wonders of the Almighty, the four Zoas. But before perfect union can be attained, all the nations must yet undergo a final harvest and vintage to make the Bread and Wine of Eternity, which will take seven days, reminiscent of the seven days of Genesis. Urizen sows the immortal souls as seed on the wide universal field, and afterwards he, with his sons, reaps the harvest, threshes and winnows the corn, by which the chaff is blown into the sea of Tharmas, the sea of time and space. Then the vintage takes place and at last Urthona grinds the corn and makes the bread of ages. Urizen is united again to Ahania, who from "her darksome cave issued in majesty divine." Luvah and Vala are restored to

[1] *The four Zoas* IX, 2, 56—62.
[2] *Ibid.*, 5, 187—192.
[3] *Ibid.* IX, 7, 267—270.

their former state and enjoy once more the bliss of Paradise. In the end Tharmas and Enion are also united there as little children. The song that Vala sings in her happiness of regained harmony is one of Blake's most beautiful pieces of poetry. It is reminiscent of the *Songs of Innocence*. The pastoral tranquillity, the charm of innocence, the pious gladness, the idyllic love of nature, which inspired these poems, also animate this jubilant hymm of the sinless soul. We sometimes even find the same images in it, but there is here an indefinable exaltation of feeling ringing in the clear melody of its solemnly ecstatic rhythm, which we did not hear in the songs of the child's Eden. Echoes of the pure love-idyll which Milton made of his description of Adam and Eve in Paradise ring through this charming pastoral; the mystic love of nature, which made St. Francis of Assisi sing of his brother the sun, of his sister the moon, sounds in the rapturous song of Vala, which she sings to the Lord, when beholding the glory of Eden:

"For in my bosom a new song arises to the Lord:

'Rise up, O sun! most glorious minister and light of day!
Flow on, ye gentle airs, and bear the voice of my rejoicing!
Wave freshly, clear waters, flowing around the tender grass;
And thou, sweet smelling ground, put forth thy life in fruit and flowers!'
Follow me, O my flocks, and hear me sing my rapturous song!
I will cause my voice to be heard on the clouds that glitter in the sun.
I will call, and who shall answer me? I will sing; who shall reply?
For from my pleasant hills behold the living, living springs
Running among my green pastures, delighting among my trees!
I am not here alone: my flocks, you are my brethren;
And you birds, that sing and adorn the sky, you are my sisters.
I sing, and you reply to my song; I rejoice, and you are glad.
Follow me, O my flocks! we will now descend into the valley." [1]

Here we have Blake at his best, and the poet-mystic, who sings out in this song the clear music of his soul, perhaps touches deeper depths of spirit than when he entangles himself and his readers in the obscure labyrinths of mystic systems.

After the uniting of the Zoas all redeemed spirits feast at the feast of Eternity, where the wine and the bread of life is taken. Urthona, the universal spirit, is no longer the spectre of Los.

[1] *The four Zoas* IX, 12, 431—445.

In unison with Enitharmon he attains to his first and harmonious state. The poetry with which Los comforted man in his fallen condition no longer exists, now that the latter has risen to eternal life, which does not consist in a desireless Nirvana, but the joy of "intellectual warfare" remains, so that it is one of exhanced and purified vitality.

> "Urthona rises from the ruinous Walls
> In all his ancient strength, to form the golden armour of science
> For intellectual War. The war of swords departed now;
> The dark religions are departed; and sweet science reigns." [1]

In *Milton* the redemption is symbolised in the figure of the poet of that name, who descends from the world of the eternals to the earth, in order to be united to his six-fold-emanation, to his three wives and three daughters, with whom he had not lived in perfect harmony on earth. [2] This breach between Milton and his emanation represents the influence of Puritanism, of Urizen-Jehovah, which he underwent. Now he sacrifices himself in order tot redeem his emanation; he is going to die the mystical death, and he is to experience that by so doing he shall find his true life. The virgin Ololon, who is troubled in heart by the descending of Milton into the land of death, follows him into the lower regions. Jesus admonished her: "Watch over this World and with your brooding wings renew to eternal life. Lo! I am with you always." She is the immortal form of Milton's mortal six-fold emanation. She comes to Blake, when he is walking one day in his cottage-garden at Felpham. "Knowest thou of Milton who descended driven from Eternity? I come him to seek." And at her question he whom she is looking for appears as a wonderful, mysterious apparition.

> "Descending down into my Garden, a Human Wonder of God,
> Reaching from heaven to earth, a Cloud and Human Form,
> I beheld Milton with astonishment." [3]

And at the same time his errors are revealed to Blake. But the

---

[1] *The four Zoas* IX, 23, 850—853.
[2] See Foster Damon, *William Blake, etc.*, p. 404.
[3] *Milton* II, 37, 13—15.

former, conscious of the importance of his mission, firmly fights against them in the person of Satan, the founder of churches and of priests, the destroyer of imaginative life, and puts off in self-annihilation all that is not of God alone;" "bathing in the waters of life, he washes off the not human." He comes

> "To cast off Rational Demonstration by Faith in the Saviour,
> To cast off the rotten rags of Memory by Inspiration,
> To cast off Bacon, Locke and Newton, from Albion's covering,
> To take off his filthy garments and clothe him with Imagination;
> To cast aside from Poetry all that is not Inspiration." [1]

Ololon in her turn sacrifices herself, and is lost in Milton's shadow "as a dove upon the stormy sea." Then Jesus appeared, enwrapped in Ololon, as in a garment. He wept and walked forth

> "From Felpham's Vale clothèd in Clouds of blood, to enter into
> Albion's Bosom, the bosom of death: and the Four surrounded him
> In the Column of Fire in Felpham's Vale; then to their mouths the Four
> Applied their four Trumpets, and then sounded to the Four winds." [2]

Blake experiences this supreme moment of the ultimate union of man with the Divine as an entire loss of earthly and bodily consciousness.

> "Terror-struck in the Vale I stood, at that immortal sound.
> My bones trembled, I fell outstretch'd upon the path
> A moment, and my Soul return'd into its mortal state
> To Resurrection and Judgment in the Vegetable Body." [3]

Immediately the lark mounted with a loud trill from Felpham's vale and the wild thyme's odour spread over Wimbledon's green hills.

A single moment did this purely mystical trance last; in a single moment the vision was seen, for, and here we have again the great mystic thought which I discussed on page 65 and following:

> "Every Time less than a pulsation of the artery
> Is equal in its period and value to Six Thousand Years.
> For in this Period the Poet's Work is Done; and all the Great

---

[1] *Milton* II, 43, 3—9.
[2] *Ibid.* II, 44, 19—23.
[3] *Ibid.*, 24—29.

> Events of Time start forth and are conceived in such a Period,
> Within a Moment, a Pulsation of the Artery!" [1]
>
> "There is a Moment in each Day that Satan cannot find,
> Nor can his Watch Fiends find it; but the Industrious find
> This Moment, and it multiply: and when it once is found,
> It renovates every Moment of the Day if rightly placèd:
> In this Moment Ololon descended." [2]

I have tried to draw from the *Prophetic Books* the essential mystical element which lies at the root of Blake's thought. We see that though clothed in different forms, the fundamental inspiration of the three *Prophetic Books* which I have been discussing, is the same; that the great vision which Blake saw shining, whether it is symbolised as the union of Albion and Jerusalem, of Urthona and Enitharmon, of Milton and Ololon, was man in union with the Divine.

---

[1] *Milton* I, 27, 28, 62—63, 1—4.
[2] *Ibid.* II, 35, 42—47.

CHAPTER IX

NATURE

The word nature had different meanings for Blake. In one sense it represented for him the great delusion, Satan, the creation of Urizen, the world of Ulro(error), which shall be burned up at the Judgment-Day, vanish into Non-entity. In another sense it denoted the living garment of God, the symbol of the All. The essence of his seemingly contradictory statements is probably the belief in nature being the reflex of the spiritual world, which the visionary sees shining in and through her transparent form, the effect of the causes that work in supernature, [1] only visible throught the imagination. Blake's conception of nature and the imagination are closely related, so that a discussion of his vision of the former will be inevitably interwoven with an exposition of his view on the latter.

Nature, without vital reality blowing its breath of life into the multiform shape of her being, or rather without the reality moulding her bodily form, [2] symbolizing itself into her, is dead, dead as Albion, who shuts his soul against the inflowing of the spirit of God. It is the nature, to speak with Blake's own words, "which has no supernatural and dissolves." [3] It depends on the way of seeing of the seer, how nature will present itself to him. "For the eye altering alters all." "A fool sees not the same tree that a wise man sees." "A wise man will know that eternity is in love with the productions of time." "If the doors of perception were cleansed everything would appear to man, as it is, infinite." [4]

---

[1] See n. 154 of Swedenborg's *Angelic Wisdom concerning divine Love*.
[2] *The Marriage of Heaven and Hell, The Voice of the Devil*.
[3] *Address of the Ghost of Abel to Lord Byron*.
[4] *The Marriage of Heaven and Hell, Proverbs of Hell*.

"I question not my corporeal eye any more than I would question a window concerning a sight. I look through it and not with it." [1]

>"We are led to believe a lie
>When we see not through the eye
>Which was born in a night, to perish in a night,
>When the Soul slept in beams of light." [2]

And the man who sees through, not with the eye, is the man of imagination. "I see everything I paint in this world, but everybody does not see alike. To the eyes of a Miser a Guinea is more beautiful than the Sun, and a bag worn with the use of money has more beautiful proportions than a vine filled with grapes. The tree which moves some to tears of joy is in the eyes of others only a Green thing that stands in the way. Some see Nature all Ridicule and Deformity, and by these I shall not regulate my proportions, and some scarce see nature at all. But to the eyes of the Man of Imagination Nature is Imagination itself." [3] This last statement is the highest praise which could be bestowed on Nature by the devoted worshipper of the imagination. "The man of imagination sees the infinite in all, sees God, but he who sees the Ratio only sees himself only." "The old prophets of Israel possessed the imaginative power in a very high degree, and therefore nature was to them alive with the Divine. The God who spoke to them was the Infinite which their senses discovered in everything, they did not see Him, nor heard Him in a finite organical perception." [4]

To the man of imagination everything touches the land of God:

>"The bleat, the bark, bellow and roar
>Are waves that beat on Heaven's shore." [5]

The meanest thing is charged with the mystery of His omnipresence. He sees "a world in a grain of sand, a Heaven in a wild flower." [6]

In him the truth lives that "God is in the lowest effects as well

---

[1] *The Vision of the last Judgment.*
[2] *Auguries of Innocence,* 125—129.
[3] *Letter to Dr. Trusler,* Aug. 23, 1799.
[4] *The Marriage of Heaven and Hell, A memorable Fancy.*
[5] *Auguries of Innocence,* 69—71.
[6] *Ibid.,* 1—3.

as in the highest causes, that he is become a man in order to nourish the weak, that creation is God descending according to the weakness of man, that everything on earth is the word of God and in its essence is God. [1] Here we have the one fact of Christ's incarnation widened into a universal phenomenon of mystical self-sacrifice.

"Since Christ, for the Christian philosopher, is Divine Life Itself — the drama of Christianity but expressing this fact and its implications 'in a point' — it follows that His active spirit is to be discerned, not symbolically, but in the most veritable sense, in the ecstatic and abounding life of the world. In the rapturous vitality of the birds, in their splendid glancing flight: in the swelling of buds and the sacrificial beauty of the flowers: in the great and solemn rhythms of the sea — there is somewhat of Bethlehem in all these things, somewhat too of Calvary in their self-giving pains. It was this re-discovery of Nature's Christliness which Blake desired so passionately when he sang —

> 'I will not cease from mental fight,
> Nor shall my sword sleep in my hand,
> Till we have built Jerusalem
> In England's green and pleasant land.'" [2]

We possess personal testimonies of nature's influence on Blake's inner life, of his enhanced visionary power through her, in a poem written to Mrs. Flaxman after his first visit to Felpham, in a letter to Mr. Flaxman, written after the poet's settlement there, and in some poems addressed to Mr. Butts during his stay in the country. To Mrs. Flaxman he described Felpham as a place visited by celestial spirits, the angelic souls of the departed, who descended along a Jacob's ladder from Heaven to earth and made

> "the bread of sweet thought and the wine of delight
> Feed the village of Felpham by day and by night. [3]

In a letter to Flaxman he says: "Felpham is a sweet place for study, because it is more spiritual than London. Heaven opens

---

[1] *Note* on Lavater's *Aphorisms*.
[2] Evelyn Underhill, *Mysticism*, pp. 138, 139.
[3] *To Mrs. Flaxman*, in a letter from Mrs. Blake to Mrs. Flaxman, 14 Sept. 1800.

here on all sides her golden gates: her windows are not obstructed by vapours; voices of celestial inhabitants are more distinctly heard, and their forms more distinctly seen." [1]

The poem written to Thomas Butts [2] is very important as being the description of the most perfect mystic vision, called forth by the sight of nature. It appeared to him one day by the seaside, when the world lay overflooded in the glory of the morning-sun. His mind was so enraptured by the wonder of light that his human feelings sunk away into the immensity of the luminous marvel.

> "Over sea, over land,
> My eyes did expand
> Into regions of air
> Away from all care;
> Into regions of fire,
> Remote from desire;
> The light of the morning
> Heaven's mountains adorning:
> In particles bright
> The jewels of light
> Distinct shone and clear."

In this fragment with the suggestive lilt in the abrupt couplets Blake reveals an experience which is not different from what many poets have felt amidst the beauty of nature. But what follows we might call peculiarly Blakean:

> "Amaz'd and in fear
> I each particle gazèd,
> Astonish'd, amazèd;
> For each was a Man,
> Human-form'd. Swift I ran,
> For they beckon'd to me,
> Remote by the sea,
> Saying: 'Each grain of sand,
> Every stone on the land,
> Each rock and each hill,
> Each fountain and rill,
> Each herb and each tree,
> Mountain, hill, earth and sea,

---

[1] *Letter to Flaxman*, Sept. 21st, 1800.
[2] In a letter of Oct. 2nd, 1800.

NATURE

> Cloud, meteor, and star,
> Are men seen afar.'"

This is the expression of the typically Blakean conception of man being the prototype of everything. His belief was that "Man can have no idea of anything greater than Man as a cup cannot contain more than its capaciousness." [1]

It is his spirit which reflects itself in nature, she is seen in the mirror of his mind. "A fool sees not the same tree that a wise man sees." [2] And this fact is symbolically expressed by him in all the forms of nature assuming the human shape. But his vision had not yet reached its ultimate form in this. As his mind penetrated deeper into the sight before him, all the separate men were united into One, the Universal Man, Christ, who, as the good Shepherd, enfolded him in His "sun-bright bosom," thus taking him up into the morning's beatitude of the child's Paradise. The ultimate union is attained here through the imaginative power enkindled at the beauty of nature. We can call Blake a nature-mystic here, who reaches the highest, the four-fold vision. The mentioning of the four-fold vision leads me to the discussion of another poem to Thomas Butts, in which Blake speaks about the four kinds of vision. When after a serious mental struggle against worldly powers, in this poem symbolized by Los, the creator of Time, who threatens the poet with poverty, if the latter should decide to leave Felpham and his patron Hayley, a struggle, in which Blake, idealism, is victorious over Los. materialism, all nature is transformed in the glow of his inspiration. Then he says:

> "Now I a fourfold vision see,
> And a fourfold vision is given to me,
> 'T is fourfold in my supreme delight,
> And threefold in soft Beulah's night
> And twofold always — May God us keep
> From single vision and Newton's sleep." [3]

Foster Damon explains the single vision as being pure sensation, such as the scientists (Newton in particular) cultivate, twofold vision added an intellectual appreciation of the object; threefold infused the perception with its emotional value and fourfold

---
[1] *Marginalia* to Swedenborg's *Angelic Wisdom concerning divine Love.*
[2] *The Marriage of Heaven and Hell, Proverbs of Hell.*
[3] In a letter to Butts from Felpham, Nov. 22, 1802.

crowned it with mystical insight as to its place in the universe. These four divisions correspond to the Four Zoas, Tharmas guiding single vision, Urizen twofold, Luvah threefold and Urthona (Los) the fourfold.[1]

I doubt whether Foster Damon is quite right in his explanation. I should be inclined to think that Tharmas, the Zoa, who presides over the careless existence of the child in its state of innocence is not the one who inspires the scientist. I am inclined to think that Urizen would sooner be the Zoa whose influence is felt in the scientist's vision. Moreover, the question suggests itself to me whether in the development of the vision last-mentioned we have not first the single vision, the simple sensuous imbibing of outward things, then the emotional perception, after that the spiritual insight, the illuminative state, when man is conscious of his relation to the cosmos, and finally the complete penetration, the perfect union. The third state, that of spiritual insight, would correspond to the vision, seen in the soft night of Beulah, a super-terrestrial region, nearest to the world of eternity, entirely surrounding it, so that everybody who ascends from the earth has to pass it on his way to the eternal realms. It is the land of contemplative life, where in the vision of Jerusalem Blake sees St. Theresa, Madame Guyon, Fénélon, Whitefield and Hervey amongst the "gentle souls" that guard the four-fold gate and guide the great wine-press of love. It is also the land of the emanations, of man's tender and quiet joys.

The vision of Tharmas, of the child of the songs of innocence, is in essence the same as the highest, the fourfold vision, with this difference that the first is unconscious, because a divided existence is unknown, the second not, because it has been reached through the state of experience.

Blake's visionary seeing of nature became less in his later years, but yet the *Prophetic Books* are shot through with glimpses of her sacramental meaning. In *Milton* the poet expresses it in a very suggestive way, with an illusion of superhumanity, what meaning he reads in the visible world. To him it is the medium through which he travels in Eternity:

[1] Foster Damon, *William Blake etc.*, p. 303. See also W. N. Guthrie, *The Sewanee Review* V, Oct. 1897.

"And all this Vegetable World appear'd on my left Foot
As a bright sandal form'd immortal of precious stones and gold.
I stoopèd down and bound it on to walk forward thro' Eternity." [1]

The gorgeously clothed flies that dance and sport upon the sunny brooks and meadows, the trees on the mountains, the thundering wind through the darksome sky, the constellations in the deep and wondrous night, which move on their immortal courses, the glittering streams, all of them reflect the Vision of Beatitude.

"But we see only as it were the hem of their garments,
When with our vegetable eyes we view these wondrous visions. [2]"

Though it is not expressive of the ultimate union, the very finest testimony of the impassioned inspiration with which nature could animate him, is the *Song of Spring* in *Milton*, where with one mighty swing we are thrown into the heart of nature, which is flooded with the precious perfume of a multitude of flowers, where all is awed into silence, where even the sun stands still to listen to the jubilant song of the lark, who "springing from the waving cornfield" mounts "on wings of light into the Great Expanse," till the whole choir of the day begins to break into music of love and adoration, awaking the sun from her "sweet reverie."

"Thou hearest the Nightingale begin the Song of Spring.
The Lark sitting upon his earthy bed, just as the morn
Appears, listens silent; then springing from the waving Corn-field, loud
He leads the Choir of Day, trill! trill! trill! trill!
Mounting upon the wings of light into the Great Expanse,
Re-echoing against the lovely blue and shining heavenly Shell.
His little throat labours with inspiration; every feather
On throat and breast and wings vibrates with the effluence Divine. [3]

. . . .

Thou perceivest the Flowers put forth their precious Odours;
And none can tell how from so small a center comes such sweet,
Forgetting that within that Center Eternity expands
Its ever during doors." [4]

It is not only one of the finest, if not the very finest lyric written

[1] *Milton* I, 19, 12—15.
[2] *Ibid.*, 26, 11—13.
[3] *Ibid.* II, 31, 28—36.
[4] *Ibid.*, 31, 46—49.

by Blake, but it is among the most impassioned songs in the whole range of English literature. Ignoring that it is a lamentation of Beulah over the loss of Ololon, we see it as pure poetry, without any obscurity of mystic symbolism. And this pure poetry is a clear example of how very near poetry and mysticism are to each other, how in essence they may be the same, how from the fullness of the poetic passion can stream the flow of soul which debouches on the boundless ocean of the All. Everything in that bright spring-dawn is athrill with the vital pulsation of the great, sweet Heart. The senses of man drink in the imaginative beauty of God's life. Nature has become here the imagination of God Himself and also of man. Blake so often argues about the divinity of the imagination, of the poetic power, but here he proves it by singing a delightful song from the abundance of his inspired heart. When writing it, he was an initiate in what in mystical literature is called the illuminative stage, where the mystic sees all illuminated by divine light.

In the discussion of this piece of poetry, also of the poem to Butts, I have partly refuted Symons's statement: "Other poets found ecstacy in nature, but Blake only in imagination."[1]

And this poet, who could thus be absorbed in the jubilee of nature, who could be inspired by her into the vision of the universal imagination, could write at another time: "I assert for myself, that I do not behold the outward creation and that to me it is hindrance and not action. It is as the 'dirt upon my feet — no part of me.'" He lets it be followed up by: "'What? it will be questioned, 'when the sun rises, do you not see a round disk of fire, something like a guinea?' Oh no! no! I see an innumerable company of the heavenly host crying: 'Holy, holy, holy, is the Lord Almighty.' I question not my corporeal eye any more than I would question a window concerning a sight. I look through it and not with it."[2] The difference between the passage in *Milton* and this utterance is that in the former he expresses the divinity of nature in terms which approach the unembodied ecstacy, in the latter he materializes the spiritual sensation. In both the revealing of the spirit is the object of the poet. "His dread of nature was partly

---

[1] Symons, *William Blake*, p. 65.
[2] *Vision of the last Judgment.*

the recoil of his love. He feared to be entangled in the veils of Vala, the seductive sight of the world of the senses, and his love of natural things is evident on every page of even the latest of *The Prophetic Books*. [1]

The fault of Blake is that in his great fear of getting lost in the illusory materialism of nature he tries to ignore her, and thus to attain to a higher spiritualism, but by so doing is apt to materialize the spiritual, though in a superhuman bodily form. "He was a too literal realist of imagination, as others are of nature." [2]

Both his poetry and his art are often a proof of his and man's inability to loosen himself entirely from earthly bonds. Involuntarily I think of a little water-colour in the Tate-gallery. It is one of Blake's finest things, a simple sketch of a view of the village of Felpham, naturalistic, and yet visionary, mystic, because the diaphanous luminosity that vibrates in its liquid colours is the interpretation of the poet's imagination, not condemnable, because made visible in forms of nature. It is more "visionary" than many symbolic representations of his heavenly or hellish visions. In rejecting nature Blake often commits the great mistake of suppressing his natural emotion to substitute it for an intellectual exposition of the value of the imagination, forgetting that an explanation of life is not life itself. He frequently embodies an inner experience in visible supernatural form, which is often less beautiful, less convincing than that which his purified senses perceive, thus affording the proof that in trying to overleap nature, of which man himself forms part, he only grasps an inferior form of her. De Sélincourt says in connection with the above-mentioned interpretation of the sunrise: "If I see angels, when the sun comes up, the angels, perhaps, are better than the sun; but that will depend, as Blake himself would say, upon the eye that sees them; many would prefer to see a sunrise with Turner rather than with Blake and would find its reality not less unchanging in eternal, and far less monotonous in temporal aspects; while the use of the imagination, though it would operate differently in each case, would be equally essential in either." [3]

---

[1] Symons, *William Blake*, p. 127.
[2] Yeats, *Ideas of Good and Evil*, p. 182.
[3] De Selincourt, *William Blake*, p. 85.

Chapter X

HIS VISIONS

A study of Blake's mysticism would not be complete, if it left his "visions" out of discussion. They make him that enigmatic figure, shrouded in a veil of mystery, standing alone as he does in the uniqueness of his inspiration and of the imaging of it. His visionary power may be traced back to a very early age. His first vision appeared to him, when he was four years old. Crabb Robinson reports Kate, Blake's exquisite, devoted wife, saying to her husband: "You know dear, the first time you saw God was when you were four years old and He put his head to the window and set you a-screaming." [1] There is an irresistable charm in the matter-of-factness with which this miraculous incident is told. It shines with Kate's implicit belief in her exceptional husband. We are not told in what shape the vision presented itself, but, as Berger suggests, it must have been something vague, as he described it afterwards in that beautiful song of *The little Boy lost*, "like his father, in white." When he was about eight, another sight of the superterrestrial world flashed in upon him. It was in one of his favourite rambles in the country near London. Peckham Rye on Dulwich Hill was the exact place where it happened. "He looks up and sees a tree filled with angels, bright angelic wings bespangling every bough like stars. Returned home, he relates the incident, and only through his mother's intercession escapes a thrashing from his honest father, for telling a lie. Another time, one summer morn, he sees the haymakers at work, and amid them angelic figures walking." [2] The prophet Ezekiel also appeared to him one day, when he was sitting under a green tree. "The

---

[1] Crabb Robinson, *Reminiscences*.
[2] Gilchrist, *The Life of William Blake*, pp. 7, 8.

Ezekiel-story is interesting as showing Blake's home atmosphere at the time. He must have been very early and very deeply impressed by the name and personality of Ezekiel. The impression never died away, but grew fruitful as time went on. We saw that in the great works of his mystical period a whole system of poetic philosophy turns on the story of four living creatures, which he tells us, were the same that Ezekiel saw by Chebar's flood." [1]

These early visions may be easily explained as arising from the strong phantasy of an exceptionally sensitive child, moved, in its first overwhelming power, by the beauty of the old Biblical stories, which through their great imaginative force are apt to lead a receptive child into the spiritual land. But the peculiarity with Blake is that visions continued to illumine him in after years and then "the grown man believed as unaffectedly in them as ever had the boy of ten." [2]

A vision of a different kind is given in the striking insight into character, or the prophetic glimpse which he showed in refusing to be apprenticed to the engraver Ryland, then the most famous and esteemed man in the sphere of engraving. "Father," said little Blake, after the two had left Ryland's studio, "I do not like the man's face: it looks as if he will live to be hanged." [3]

Twelve years afterwards he committed a forgery and little Blake's words came true.

What had a great formative influence on Blake's mind was his being daily in Westminster-Abbey for some period of time during his apprenticeship with Basire. His master sent him there in order to make drawings from the ancient memorials. The lonely communion with the spirit of past ages in the shadowy splendour of the Abbey awakened the visionary power in him. Daily living amidst "the regal forms, which for five centuries had lain in mute majesty, — once amid the daily presence of reverent priest and muttered mass, since in awful solitude, — around the lovely Chapel of the Confessor: the austere sweetness of Queen Eleanor, the dignity of Philippa, the noble grandeur of Edward the Third,

[1] Ellis and Yeats, *William Blake etc.* II, p. 7.
[2] Gilchrist, *The Life of William Blake*, p. 8.
[3] *Ibid.*, p. 13.

the gracious stateliness of Richard II and his Queen, ... shut up alone with these solemn memorials of far-off centuries, ... the Spirit of the past became his familiar companion. Sometimes his dreaming eye saw more palpable shapes from the phantom past: once a vision of 'Christ and the Apostles.'" [1] This vision closes the period of Blake's youth.

When in 1787 his brother Robert died, whom he had nursed with the utmost love and tenderness for fourteen days and nights at a stretch, he saw the released soul ascending to Heaven, clapping his hands for joy. On page 9 I spoke about the message which his departed brother sent him.

At Felpham the visions were very frequent. The tranquillity of the country seemed to be conducive to the raising of the spiritual sights. In a poem *To Thomas Butts* he speaks of "silver angels" and "golden devils," of the souls of the departed hovering around him in the trees, the fields and the clouds in the Felpham-country.

> "With Happiness stretch'd across the hills
> In a cloud that dewy sweetness distils;
> With a blue sky spread over with wings,
> And a mild sun that mounts and sings;
> With trees and fields full of fairy elves,
> And little devils who fight for themselves —
> . . . .
> With angels planted in hawthorn bowers,
> And God Himself in the passing hours;
> With silver angels across my way,
> And golden demons that none can stay;
> With my father hovering upon the wind,
> And my brother Robert just behind,
> And my brother John, the evil one,
> In a black cloud making his moan, —
> Tho' dead, they appear upon my path." [2]

It was also at Felpham that he saw one day the funeral of a fairy. " 'Did you ever see a fairy's funeral, madam?', he once said to a lady who happened to sit by him in company. 'Never sir,' was the answer. 'I have!' said Blake, 'but not before last night. I was walking alone in my garden; there was a great stillness among

---

[1] Gilchrist, *The Life of William Blake*, p. 18.
[2] In a letter to Butts from Felpham, Nov. 22, 1802.

the branches and flowers and more than common sweetness in the air; I heard a low and pleasant sound, and I knew not whence it came. At last, I saw the broad leaf of a flower move and underneath I saw a procession of creatures, of the size and colour of green and grey grasshoppers, bearing a body laid out on a rose leaf, which they buried with songs and then disappeared. It was a fairy funeral!" [1] Sometimes he held visionary conversations with the great spirits of the past, with the Prophets, Homer, Dante, Milton, all "majestic shadows, grey but luminous, and superior to the common heights of men." [2] Crabb Robinson tells us when Blake spoke of Milton appearing to him: "I asked whether he resembled the prints of him and he answered: 'All.' 'Of what age?' 'Various ages — sometimes a very old man.'" [3] In another place Crabb Robinson says: "I asked in what language Voltaire spoke — 'To my sensation it was English. It was like the touch of a musical key. He touched it probably French, but to my ear it became English.' I asked why he did not draw the spirits. 'It is not worth while. There are so many, the labour would be too great. As to Shakespeare, he is exactly like the old engraving which is called a bad one. I think it very good.'" [4]

Most peculiar are the visions which he had in the presence of John Varley, a landscape-painter and astrologer. "Varley it was who encouraged Blake to take authentic sketches of certain among his most frequent spiritual visitants. The Visionary faculty was so much under control, that, at the wish of a friend, he could summon before his abstracted gaze any of the familiar forms and faces he was asked for. This was during the favourable and befitting hours of night; from nine or ten in the evening, until one or two, or perhaps three and four o'clock, in the morning; Varley sitting by, 'sometimes slumbering and sometimes waking.' Varley would say, 'Draw me Moses, or David;' or would call for a likeness of Julius Caesar, or Cassibellaunus, or Edward the Third, or some other great historical personage. Blake would

---

[1] Cunningham, *The Life of William Blake*, quoted by Gilchrist in *The Life of William Blake*, pp. 162, 163.
[2] *Ibid.*, p. 162.
[3] Crabb Robinson, *Diary*, 17 Dec., 1825.
[4] *Ibid.*, 18 Febr., 1826.

answer, 'There he is!' and paper and pencil being at hand, he would begin drawing with the utmost alacrity and composure, looking up from time to time as though he had a real sitter before him; ingenuous Varley, meanwhile, straining wistful eyes into vacancy and seeing nothing, though he tried hard, and at first expected his faith and patience to be rewarded by a genuine apparition. A 'vision' had a very different signification with Blake to that it had in literal Varley's mind.

Sometimes Blake had to wait for the Vision's appearance; sometime it would come at call. At others, in the midst of his portrait, he would suddenly leave off, and, in his ordinary quiet tones and with the same matter-of-fact air another might say 'It rains,' would remark, 'I can't go on, — it is gone! I must wait till it returns'; or 'It has moved. The mouth is gone'; or 'he frowns; he is displeased with my portrait of him': which seemed as if the Vision were looking over the artist's shoulder as well as sitting *vis-à-vis* for his likeness. The devil himself would politely sit in a chair to Blake, and innocently disappear; which obliging conduct one would hardly have anticipated from the spirit of evil, with his well-known character for love of wanton mischief.

In sober daylight criticisms were hazarded by the profane on the character or drawing of these or any of his visions. 'Oh! it's all right!' Blake would calmly reply; 'it must be right. I saw it so.' It did not signify what you said; nothing could put him out: so assured was he that he, or rather his imagination, was right, and that what the latter revealed was implicitly to be relied on, — and this without any appearance of conceit or intrusiveness on his part. Yet critical friends would trace in all these heads the Blake mind and hand, his *receipt* for a face: every artist has his own, his favourite idea, from which he may depart in the proportions, but seldom substantially. John Varley, however, could not be persuaded to look at them from this merely rationalistic point of view.[1] To the visionary pictures painted for Varley also belongs the well-known "ghost of a flea." Varley tells about it: "I called on Blake one evening and found him more than usually excited. He told me he had seen a wonderful thing — the ghost of a flea! 'And did you make a drawing of him?' I inquired. 'No,

[1] Gilchrist, *The Life of William Blake*, pp. 271, 272, 273.

indeed,' said he. 'I wish I had, but I shall, if he appears again.' He looked earnestly into a corner of the room and then said, 'here he is, reach me my things — I shall keep my eye on him. Here he comes, his eager tongue whisking out of his mouth, a cup in his hand to hold blood and covered with a skaly skin of gold and green' — as he described him, so he drew him." [1] He told Butts that he had written Milton "from immediate dictation, twelve or sometimes twenty or thirty lines at a time, without premeditation, and even against my will. The time it has taken in writing was thus rendered non-existent, and an immense poem exists which seems to be the labour of a long life, all produced without labour or study." [2] In another letter he said: "I may praise it, since I dare not pretend to be other than the secretary; the authors are in eternity. [3] In another letter to Butts he wrote: "I feel neither shame, nor fear, nor repugnance, in telling you that night and day I am under the direction of messengers from Heaven." [4] To Crabb Robinson he said: "I write, when commanded by the spirits and the moment I have written I see the words fly about the room in all directions." [5]

His happiest and most beautiful vision was his last, in which the light of the eternal day began to dawn, when the pilgrim was reaching "the country he had all his life wished to see." "Just before he died his countenance became fair, his eyes brightened and he burst out into singing of the things he saw in Heaven." To his loving Catherine, of whom he had testified that she had been the angel of his life he said of the songs he sang: "My beloved! they are not mine. No! they are not mine." [6]

The great question is how we have to look upon these visions, whether they are objective images of spiritual beings, spiritual regions, having an existence outside the seer, or whether they are to be considered as the visible projection of the mystic's mind. The latter conception is the most usual. His earliest

[1] Cunningham, *The Life of William Blake*, reprinted in Symons, *William Blake*, p. 422.
[2] *Letter to Butts*, 25 April, 1803.
[3] *Ibid.*, 6 July, 1803.
[4] *Ibid.*, 10 Jan., 1802.
[5] Crabb Robinson, *Diary*, 18 Febr. 1826.
[6] Gilchrist., *The Life of William Blake*, pp. 382, 381.

biographer, J. T. Smith, says: "Blake was supereminently endowed with the power of disuniting all other thoughts from his mind, whenever he wished to indulge in thinking of any particular subject, and so firmly did he believe, by this abstracting power, that the objects of his compositions were before him in his mind's eye that he frequently believed them to be speaking to him." [1] Another biographer has a similar opinion: "His not earning fame, etc. had the consequence of his becoming more seriously thoughtful, he avoided the company of men, and lived in the manner of a hermit in that vast wilderness London. He was thus compelled more than ever to retire to worlds of his own creating, and seek solace in visions of paradise for the joys which the earth denied him. By frequent indulgence in these imaginings he gradually began to believe in the reality of what dreaming fancy painted — the pictured forms which swarmed before his eyes assumed in his apprehension the stability of positive revelations, and he mistook the vivid figures, which his professional imagination shaped, for the poets, and heroes and princes of old." [2] "His fancy overmastered him — until he at length confounded the mind's eye with the corporeal organ and dreamed himself out of the sympathies of actual Life." [3]

Reference has been made to what Gilchrist thought about the question in connection with Varley's visionary drawings. Charles Lamb, writing to Bernard Barton about Blake said: "He paints in water-colours marvelloous strange pictures, visions of his brain, which he asserts that he has seen." [4] Otto von Taube in his beautiful essay on Blake expresses himself on this subject in a similar spirit. "Die Visionen hatten aber nichts gemein mit den Erscheinungen wie sie heute der Spiritismus glaubt und wie sie mit Recht oder Unrecht Swedenborg, aber auch Blake nachgesagt werden. [5] Symons very strongly defends Blake against those who would reckon him amongst the spiritualists and magicians. "He saw vi-

---

[1] J. T. Smith, *Nollekens and His Times*, reprinted in Symons, *William Blake*, p. 363.
[2] Cunningham, *The Life of William Blake*, reprinted in Symons, *William Blake*, p. 401.
[3] *Ibid.*, p. 430.
[4] The Works of Charles and Mary Lamb, *Letters*, pp. 642, 643.
[5] Otto von Taube, *Die Ethik der Fruchtbarkeit*.

sions, but not as the spiritualists and the magicians have seen them. These desire to quicken mortal sight until the soul limits itself again, takes body and returns to reality, but Blake, the inner mystic, desired only to quicken that imagination, which he knew to be more real than the reality of nature. Why should he call up shadows, when he could talk in the spirit with spiritual realities? Blake wrote about it himself in the *Descriptive Catalogue*: 'The Prophets describe what they saw in vision as real and existing men, whom they saw with their imaginative and immortal organs. The Apostles the same.'" [1] In another place he compares Blake's with Shakespeare's imagination. The difference between them is that "the one has a visual imagination and sees an image or a methaphor as a literal reality, while the other seeing it not less vividly, but in a 'more purely mental way,' adds a 'like' or an 'as', and the image or methaphor comes to you with its apology or attenuation, and takes you less by surprise. But to Blake the universe was the methaphor." [2]

Greville Mac Donald also quotes Shakespeare in orde to elucidate Blake's imagination. "I believe," he says, "if we could analyse the way by which the genius works, we should find that it is simply through seeing visions. Shakespeare fathers his visions on his characters:

> 'Look how the floor of heaven
> Is thick inlaid with patiness of bright gold:
> There's not the smallest orb which thou behold'st
> But in his motion like an angel sings,
> Still quiring to the young-eyed cherubins,
> Such harmony is in immortal souls;
> But whilst this muddy vesture of decay
> Doth grossly close it in, we cannot hear it." [3]

MacDonald does not think Blake's dreams objective, first because they are not the substance that dreams are made of, secondly, because they are not the fanciful fears of the too impressionable child, thirdly, because they are not the ghosts of the superstitious or the incoherent rhapsodies of the lunatic. [4]

[1] Symons, *William Blake*, pp. 12, 13.
[2] Symons, *William Blake*, p. 20.
[3] Greville Mac Donald, *The Sanity of William Blake*, p. 49.
[4] *Ibid.*, p. 53.

We detect a slight difference in the criticisms of Symons and Mac Donald on the one hand, and Smith and Cunningham on the other. The former do not see anything in the visions of Blake but the poet's imagination, developed to a very high degree, the latter also attribute his visions to the imagination, deny objectivity to them, but, and this makes the difference, think Blake himself sometimes lived under the delusion that they were objective. We also find this different note struck among modern critics, by Stephan Zweig: "Das Wort Geist wahr ihm nicht methaphorisch, sondern substanziell. Er glaubte als Swedenborg an Geister und Engel, etc. und wurde sich nie klar darüber, dass die innere Vision nichts Transzendentes sei, sondern nur die künstlerische Vorstellung. [1]

H. N. Morris goes farther in this direction: "That Blake saw and spoke with inhabitants of the spirit-world no Swedenborg student would deny as a possibility or even probability." [2]

Evelyn Underhill says of Blake's visions: "they were 'corporeal,' and not 'imaginary' in type, and do not so much represent visualized intuitions as actual and constant perceptions of that 'real and eternal world' in which he held that it was man's privilege to dwell."

Dr. Garth Wilkinson expresses himself very strongly in this direction. He says that Cunningham has not understood his vision in calling it delusion, "yet," he adds, "it is far indeed from our intention to express any approbation of the spirit in which he conceived and executed his later works. But since every human being, even during his sojourn in the material world, is the union of a Spirit and a body, the spirit of each being among spirits in the spiritual, even as his body is among bodies in the natural world, — it is therefore plain that if the mind has unusual intuitions, which are not included by the common laws of nature and of body, and not palpable to the common eye, such intuitions must be regarded as Spiritual Facts or phenomena; and their source looked for, in the everpresent influences, — Divinely provided or permitted, according as they are for good or evil,

[1] Stephan Zweig, *Die Auferstehung William Blakes*, Neue freie Presse, 27 Jan., 1907.
[2] Morris, *Blake and Swedenborg*, The Quest XI, Oct. 1919.
[3] Evelyn Underhill, *Mysticism*, p. 335.

— of our own human predecessors, all now spiritual beings.[1]

Much is to be said for the opinion of Symons and others. I believe that a great deal of his art was a symbolic representation of spiritual experiences. The figures in the *Prophetic Books* are images born of Blake's fertile and plastic mind. In them are visualized the conceptions which he had of man, the world and God. This view is strengthened by definite sayings on the subject by Blake himself. We read Symons's quotation: "The Prophets describe what they saw in vision as real and existing men, whom they saw with their imaginative and immortal organs." When a lady who had heard him describe one of his visions asked: "I beg your pardon, Mr. Blake, but may I ask you where you saw this?" Blake answered her: "Here, Madam," touching his forehead.[2] He made a clear distinction between a ghost and a vision, the first being seen by the bodily, the second by the spiritual eye. Gilchrist says: "When talking on the subjects of ghosts, he was wont to say they did not appear much to imaginative men, but only to common minds, who did not see the finer spirits. A ghost was a thing seen by the gross bodily eye, a vision by the mental. 'Did you ever see a ghost?' asked a friend. 'Never but once,' was the reply. And it befell thus. Standing one evening at his garden-door in Lambeth and chancing to look up, he saw a horrible grim figure, 'scaly, speckled, very awful,' stalking downstairs towards him. More frightened than ever before or after he took to his heels, and ran out of the house."[3] This last incident is a proof of the general subjective character of Blake's visions, yet it does not alter the fact that it is an instance of spiritualistic sensitiveness. In connection with the experiences of his childhood, which at any rate cannot be conscious creations of his mind, it points to a spiritualistic turn.[4] I doubt, if Foster Damon is quite right, when he attributes Varley's visionary heads to Blake's wicked encouraging of the former's belief. Moreover we cannot overlook the fact that his utterance for instance to Butts about Milton being dictated

---

[1] Wilkinson, *Preface to the Songs of Innocence and Experience.*
[2] Gilchrist, *The Life of William Blake*, p. 338.
[3] *Ibid.*, p. 127.
[4] Harold Bruce considers all the reports of his youthful visions to be false. (*William Blake in this World*, p. 8.)

to him is of such a nature that it suggests a literal dictation, different from the inspiration by which every poet is inspired. It may be that Blake did not mean literally what he said, but his words have their independent meaning. Ellis and Yeats say: "It would have been practically impossible, and it is at any rate practically incredible that this (the visions) should have been the result of deliberate contrivance." .... "It may be true that outside the man was an atmosphere of visionary matter always ready to permeate him, to which from time to time he was more or less open. One brain in the same shell may have been more porous to its influence than the other. All these are matters of what may be called occult physiology. But the plainest of physiological problems are so mysterious that only metaphor will state them." [1] I cannot entirely agree with critics like Symons; I am of the same opinion as Berger, who says: „Il est extrêmement probable — et c'est notre opinion personelle — qu'il n'y avait dans ses visions aucune réalité objective, mais il est impossible d'être complètement affirmatif sur ce point. Comme dans toutes les questions, en dehors du cercle de notre expérience matérielle, il y a de la place pour la foi en toutes choses." [2] A saying of Blake's which points to independent spirits appearing to him, no creation of his own mind is on the frontispiece to *Visions of the Daughters of Albion*: "The eye sees more than the heart knows."

As to the value of visions, I draw attention to the fact that by the great mystics they are considered as revelations of doubtful worth, not belonging to the state of highest initiation, when Spirit speaks to Spirit.

And with this chapter I shall close my discussion of Blake's mysticism, but not before drawing attention to the fact that Foster Damon recognizes in the growth of Blake's mystic consciousness the five stages as distinguished by Evelyn Underhill and mentioned by me in the introduction. The first three states are named by him 'Innocence,' 'Experience' and 'Revolution.' The fourth state was passed in silence, while the fifth state was a return to 'Innocence' with the added wisdom of 'Experience.' [3] He individ-

---

[1] Ellis and Yeats, *The Works of William Blake, etc.* II, p. 95, 96.
[2] Berger, *William Blake, etc.* p. 55.
[3] Foster Damon, *William Blake etc.*, p. 2.

ually passed through these states and so does mankind as a whole, so we can also find them in the march of history through the ages. In history they are Eternity, the Fall, the Life of Christ, the eighteen Christian Centuries, the New Age. I cannot but express my opinion that the states of soul as meant by Evelyn Underhill are different from those which Blake passed through. The *Songs of Experience* are expressive of the disillusionment of manhood after the child's dream of innocence. They do not speak of a consciousness of personal sinfulness, which oppresses the mystics Evelyn Underhill alludes to. Hence an inner purgation is out of the question. Besides, the next stage, revolution, represented in history by the life of Christ, in Blake's existence by the writing of his revolutionary books, such as *The French Revolution*, *America*, is not the ordinary mystic's illumination after the purgative state. As I already observed, the life of Christ is more, infinitely more than a life of revolution. When we only see it in that way the true mystic note is lost to us.

I can only agree with Foster Damon in seeing in Blake's mysticism a vision of eternity, where man lived happy before his fall in matter, which the child still enjoys in its Eden of innocence, which man loses in the oppression of his physical life, which yet he may enjoy in moments of insight, in imaginative illumination when he is mystically united with the Source of his early bliss, and which shall be his for ever at the end of time, when the earth shall have vanished and man shall shine in the eternal body of his imagination in the land of pure spirit.

Chapter XI

WILLIAM WORDSWORTH

1770—1850

NATURE

When we now consider Wordsworth as a mystic poet, we shall see that in many respects he greatly differed from Blake. The minds of the two poets were widely divergent. Blake, the weird visionary, living in a hazy, mysterious world of angels and demons, in a vague cloudland, lying far beyond the limited ken of ordinary mortals, Blake, ignoring the world of the senses as illusion on his flight towards Reality, and Wordsworth, the realist, to whom the tangible world of the senses was a source of ever-flowing delight, of ever-luminous revelation, whose very art was born from the tie that bound him in loving communion to the external world, which delighted his eye and ear and which gladdened his heart, as it did no other poet; Blake the symbolist, representing his spiritual visions in tangible form, Wordsworth again the pure. realist, who conveyed without any intermediary of symbolism the vision of his eye and of his heart.

But in tracing the mystical element in the two poets, it will be interesting to notice that often external divergence proves to be inner unity, that in the depth they often approach and even touch each other. Their profoundest feelings, their highest experiences of ultimate things, though expressed in different ways, though clothed in different forms, often prove to be identical in essence.

Beginning to discuss Wordsworth's mysticism, I shall first deal with his conception of nature, because from the earliest beginning she was the great inspiring force of his poetry, his mysticism. His mystic view of the child, of man, of life, has its root in the revelations which nature bestowed on him in moments of emotional fullness. His name is especially attached to the highest nature-poetry England has produced, but many critics do not penetrate into the purely mystical insight of him, do not plumb the depth of the mind which in the loving communion with nature saw the Light in which all substance is exhaled into the Spirit of God. Irving Babbitt for instance has a most astonishing lack of insight into the mystical character of Wordsworth's poetry, but even those who show a keen appreciation of its spirituality, as Herford, Matthew Arnold, Stopford Brooke, or who assign a mystical element to it, as Raleigh, Myers, do not bring into prominence that the mystical inspiration was the all-predominating power of his work, that stripped of its mysticism, the most valuable part of it is gone. He more than other poets saw the whole range of life in the light of the supersensuous experience, enkindled at the sights of nature. Even Harper, whose biography is considered the authoritative work on Wordsworth, does not grasp the entire luminosity of his superterrestrial vision. Beatty, one of the latest writers on Wordsworth is strangely remote from the mystical nature of his work. Among those who have come nearest to a consummate appreciation of it are besides Legouis whose splendid book „La jeunesse de William Wordsworth," will ever remain one of the most illuminating and suggestive studies on him, Sneath, who treats him from a purely mystic point of view, and in a sense Garrod, who, though less pronounced in his opinion, states that Wordsworth's poetry is essentially mystical and gives an interpretation of it in accordance with this statement, and last not least Caroline Spurgeon, who, among literary critics, has brought most strongly to the fore the preeminently mystical character of his works.[1] She goes so far as to declare that among English writers and poets the only two who fulfil the strict definition of a mystic as a man who having direct knowledge of a truth which for him is absolute, consequently invariably acts

---

[1] It is important to note that Inge in his *Christian Mysticism*, p. 305, a book not dealing with poet-mystics, but wish Christian mysticism in general says of Wordsworth that he is unquestionably the greatest prophet of nature-mysticism.

upon this knowledge as inevitably as the blind man to whom sight had been granted, would make use of his eyes, are Wordsworth and Blake.

"Mysticism is the most salient feature of Wordsworth's poetry, for he was one who saw, whose inward eye was focussed to visions scarce dreamt of by men. It is because of the strangeness and unfamiliarity of his vision that he is a difficult poet to understand and the key to the understanding of him is a mystic one. People talk of the difficulty of Browning, but he is easy reading compared with a great deal of Wordsworth. It is just the apparent simplicity of Wordsworth's thought which is so misleading. A statement about him of the following kind would be fairly generally accepted as the truth. Wordsworth was a simple-minded poet, with a passion for nature, he found great joy and consolation in the contemplation of the beauty of hills and dales and clouds and flowers, and urged others to find this too; he lived, and recommended others to live a quiet retired unexciting kind of life, and he preached a doctrine of simplicity and austerity. Now, except that Wordsworth had a passion for Nature, there is not a single true statement here. Wordsworth was not only a poet, he was also a seer, a mystic and a practical psychologist, with an amazingly subtle mind and an unusual capacity for feeling; he lived a life of excitement and passion, and he preached a doctrine of magnificence and glory. It was not the beauty of Nature which brought him joy and peace, but the *life* in Nature. He himself had caught a vision of that life, he knew it and felt it, and it transformed the whole existence for him. He believed that every man could attain this vision which he so fully possessed, and his whole life's work took the form of a minute and careful analysis of the processes of feeling in his own nature, which he left as a guide for those who would tread the same path." [1]

In four short poems, written at Alfoxden in the spring of 1798, *Lines written in early Spring*, *To my Sister*, *Expostulation and Reply* and *The Tables turned*, Wordsworth for the first time discloses definitely his peculiarly spiritual feeling of nature. Though

---

[1] Caroline Spurgeon, *Mysticism in English Literature*, pp. 59, 60.

the highest mystical experience is not reached, yet it is suggestive of it. Upon the mind which "in wise passiveness" opens itself to her influences, nature will bestow her endless blessings. The highest wisdom sings in the song of the throstle and the linnet. The joy of the flowers, the sweetness of the air, satisfies the soul's yearning. Nature reveals man to himself. In the purity of her joy and beauty he finds his true attitude towards life. The spontaneous emotion she awakens in him bears the truth which remains hidden to the "meddling intellect of man." So Wordsworth with true mystic insight puts feeling, intuition, above reason, as being truer guides to the secret of life.

> "Books! 't is a dull and endless strife,
> Come, hear the woodland linnet,
> How sweet his music! on my life
> There's more of wisdom in it.
>
> And hark! how blithe the throstle sings!
> He, too, is no mean preacher:
> Come forth into the light of things,
> Let Nature be your Teacher.
> . . . .
> One impulse from a vernal wood
> May teach you more of man,
> Of moral evil and of good
> Than all the sages can." [1]

These verses have been considered as not seriously meant, as said in a mood of playful banter to a friend, who was too much given to study. John Morley for instance says: "It is best to he entirely sceptical as to the existence of system and ordered philosophy in Wordsworth. When he tells us that

> 'One impulse from a vernal wood
> May teach you more of man,
> Of moral evil and of good,
> Than all the sages can,'

such a proposition cannot be seriously taken as more than a half-playful sally for the benefit of some bookish friend. No impulse from a vernal wood can teach us anything at all of moral evil

---
[1] *The Tables turned.*

and of good." [1] Oscar Campbell is of the same opinion: "Wordsworth jested with Matthew, because Matthew jested with him." [2] Though I admit that a light, playful tone runs through the poem, yet I do not agree with these critics and am of opinion that they fail to grasp the essential spirit of them. My belief is that the poet was truly in earnest, and it is strengthened, when I consider that this faith in nature's moral force is the underlying principle of the greater part of his poetry. To take only one example out of many in *The Prelude*, where he speaks of books, which for their great value must ever be hallowed, the poet says:

> "only less,
> For what we are and what we may become,
> Than nature's self, which is the breath of God,
> Or His pure Word by miracle revealed." [3]

The truth of the above-mentioned lines is entirely lost on Irving Babbitt, who wishes to comprise within the limits of his vision, the endless revelations of poetic inspiration and who denounces Wordsworth's attitude towards nature in the words: "Wordsworth would have us believe that man is taught by woods and rills and not by contact with his fellow-men. He pushes the latter paradox to a point that would have made Rousseau stare and gasp, when he asserts that 'one impulse, etc.'" [4] How different is Myers's attitude towards this poem, when speaking of *Expostulation and Reply* and *The Tables turned*, he says that they are of the very essence of Wordsworth's nature and that it is hardly too much to say that if these two last-named poems — to the careless eye so slight and trifling — were all that had remained from Wordsworth's hand, they would have spoken to the comprehending of a new individuality." [5] Raleigh says: "If no impulse from a vernal wood can teach us anything at all of moral evil and of good, then Wordsworth himself can teach us nothing at all of moral evil and of good. The secret of his strength is taken

---

[1] John Morley, *Preface to his edition of Wordsworth*, quoted by Walter Raleigh, *Wordsworth*, p. 131.
[2] *Modern Language Notes*, November, 1921.
[3] *The Prelude* V, 218—222.
[4] Irving Babbitt, *Rousseau and Romanticism*, p. 33.
[5] F. W. H. Myers, *Wordsworth*, p. 33.

from him." [1] Bradley's opinion is that Raleigh has well defended these lines. [2] In another place he says that the road into Wordsworth's mind must be through his strangeness and paradoxes, not round them. [3] Henry S. Pancoast expresses a devious opinion from Oscar Campbell in an answer to the latter in the *Modern Language Notes*. [4]

I have spoken at some length about these poems and their different criticism, because the appreciation of them is essential in the general valuation of Wordsworth's nature-mysticism.

As I already observed, Wordsworth again and again expressed this belief in the moral force of nature, often finer, more convinced, and with a deeper penetration into nature's essential being. In *Lines composed a few Miles above Tintern Abbey*, one of the finest nature-poems he ever wrote, and which contains the different phases of his feeling towards nature in epitome, he declares to owe to her feelings

> "such, perhaps
> As have no slight or trivial influence
> On that best portion of a good man's life,
> His little, nameless, unremembered acts
> Of kindness and of love." [5]

He finds in her "the anchor of his purest thoughts, the nurse, the guide, the guardian of his heart, and soul of all his moral being." [6] And the spiritual elevation which he experiences in the presence of nature is owing to the fact that through her he attains to union with God. In the midst of the powers of nature he feels himself lost in the absorbing feeling of the nearness of the Divine.

> " I have felt
> A presence that disturbs me with the joy
> Of elevated thoughts; a sense sublime
> Of something far more deeply interfused,
> Whose dwelling is the light of setting suns,
> And the round ocean, and the living air,

---

[1] Walter Raleigh, *Wordsworth*, p. 134.
[2] A. C. Bradley, *Oxford Lectures on English Poetry*, p. 102.
[3] *Ibid.*, p. 101.
[4] *Modern Language Notes* XXXVII, 1922.
[5] *Tintern Abbey*, 31—35.
[6] *Ibid.*, 109—112.

>   And the blue sky, and in the mind of man:
>   A motion and a spirit, that impels
>   All thinking things, all objects of all thought,
>   And rolls through all things." [1]

He owes to her

>   "that blessed mood,
>   In which the burthen of the mystery,
>   In which the heavy and the weary weight
>   Of all this unintelligible world,
>   Is lightened: — that serene and blessed mood
>   In which the affections gently lead us on, —
>   Until, the breath of this corporeal frame
>   And even the motion of our human blood
>   Almost suspended, we are laid asleep
>   In body, and become a living soul:
>   While with an eye made quiet by the power
>   Of harmony, and the deep power of joy,
>   We see into the life of things." [2]

Here Wordsworth is the true mystic for whom the earth dwindles away in the radiance of his inner vision. Physical barriers drop before the revelations of the spirit, and he stands face to face with the Infinite, whose loving Heart he feels pulsate in the depth of things. Wordsworth has reached here the last stage on the mystic way, that of perfect union with the transcendental life. The afore-mentioned quotations lead up to this. In the four little poems the elements of his final consummation are present. They are expressive of a spiritual, moral force, felt in the joy, the love that lives in the exterior world, and which can been enjoyed by man, when his soul is in a state of "wise passiveness." This is considered by many mystics as the state of mind necessary for the initiation into the contemplative life. „Think not before what thou shalt do after," says the author of

---

[1] *Tintern Abbey*, 93—102.
[2] *Ibid.*, 37—50. There is a striking similarity, not only in thought, but also in words, between Swedenborg and Wordsworth. "The man with whom the spiritual degree has been opened comes into that wisdom when he dies, and he can also come into it by a laying asleep of the sensations of the body and by an influx into the spiritual things of his mind from above. (Angelic Wisdom concerning divine Love.)

The Cloud of Unknowing, "but forsake as well good thoughts as evil thoughts and pray not with thy mouth, but lift thee right well. And look that nothing live in thy working mind but a "naked intent stretching unto God." [1] "The disciples of St. Dionysius asked him why Timotheus surpassed them all in perfection. Then said Dionysius: 'Timotheus is receptive of God. And thus thine ignorance is not a defect, but thy highest perfection, and thine inactivity thy highest work.'" [2]

In this "naked intent stretching unto God," in the inactivity hiding the highest work, which lead the great religious mystics into the Promised Land, we recognize Wordsworth's "wise passiveness," which made him share the joyous and loving life of nature. We must guard against overlooking the little word wise, which just makes here all the difference between the true and the false psychic state, the difference, as Evelyn Underhill says, between "the tense stillness of the athlete and the limp passivity of the sluggard." [3]

In *The Prelude* Wordsworth also expresses himself clearly about the nature of the receptive state of the soul:

> "From her (nature) receives
> That energy by which he seeks the truth,
> From her that happy stillness of the mind,
> Which fits him to receive it when unsought." [4]

The first and second quotations from *Tintern Abbey* express the same belief of a moral force in nature, in the latter with a stronger conviction, a more absolute faith. In the third it is widened into a consciousness of the oneness of life hidden in the diversity of appearances. The poet sees the world illuminated by the light of a universal spirit, of which he himself forms a joyous part. The state of soul which sees the world in this light, which is conscious of an enhanced elevation of thought, is what in mystic literature is called the illuminative. This enhanced, leads to the experience of the body being laid asleep and the pure life of the

---

[1] Evelyn Underhill, *Mysticism*, p. 382.
[2] Eckhart, *Predigten* II, quoted by Evelyn Underhill in *Mysticism*, p. 383.
[3] Evelyn Underhill, *Mysticism*, p. 384.
[4] *The Prelude* XIII, 7—11.

soul entering the life of the All. Many poets, among whom Shelley, Byron, Walt Whitman, have been initiates in the illuminative stage of the mystic way, but Wordsworth went farther, and for this he is unique among English nature-poets.

That summer-evening at Hawkshead, when he was walking round the lake which bore such dear remembrances of his early delights, the poet was also moved into the supreme experience of union with God:

>"Gently did my soul
>Put off her veil, and, self-transmuted, stood
>Naked, as in the presence of her God." [1]

Wordsworth's poetry is scattered through with descriptions of similar religious ecstasies. This "blessed mood," which he owes to nature, is the key to "the healing-power" [2] of his poetry. He who has felt the thrilling touch of the central Force of Life, feels a joy leap up within him stronger than human grief. He who dives into the depth will find the gladness that makes the heart be still in the fullness of peace. He will be able in spite of "evil tongues, rash judgements, sneers of selfish men, greetings where no kindness is," in spite of "all the dreary intercourse of daily life," to maintain his cheerful faith that "all which we behold is full of blessings." [3]

Reference has been made to the fact that *Tintern Abbey* contains the expression of the different phases in Wordsworth's nature-feeling in epitome. In this poem he speaks about the time when, in the careless rapture of youth, he delighted in nature, because he delighted in the free exercise of his vigorous young body in the open air. It was the time when "like a roe" he bounded o'er the mountains by the side of deep rivers and lonely streams. In an intoxication of physical energy he threw himself into the mighty life of nature, which from all sides came rushing in upon him. "I cannot paint what then I was," he says.

>"The sounding cataract
>Haunted me like a passion: the tall rock,

[1] *The Prelude* IV, 150—153.
[2] Matthew Arnold, *Elegiac Stanzas*.
[3] *Tintern Abbey*, 128—134.

> The mountain, and the deep and gloomy wood,
> Their colours and their forms, were then to me
> An appetite; a feeling and a love,
> That had no need of a remoter charm,
> By thought supplied, or any interest
> Unborrowed from the eye." [1]

This was at the time, when he was a pupil at Hawkshead Grammar-School, a time which is gratefully remembered by him in *The Prelude*, his beautiful autobiographical poem, in which he traces his spiritual development, in which he reveals to us when and how his love of nature originated and gradually grew into that deep and mystic worship of her, which was the creative force of many of his most beautiful poems. The time Wordsworth spent at Hawkshead was perhaps the happiest and the most important period of his life. Here the poet and mystic were born in him. Here nature's education, begun at Cockermouth, his native town, was brought to the highest completion. At Cockermouth, where he lived till his eighth year he had already felt the soothing touch of nature's loveliness. The charm of the river Derwent, which flows at the back of the house of his birth, sank into the boy's receptive heart. It wove itself through the impressions of his early life. The stream blended its murmurs with his nurse's song and from its shady alders and rocky falls a voice issued that flowed along his dreams, composing his thoughts to a softness beyond that of an ordinary child, and giving him a dim earnest of the calm he was to find breathed by nature through hills and groves. It was, as he says, "fair seed-time for his soul," and he grew up "fostered by beauty." [2]

After the death of his mother, to whose tranquil, pious personality he testifies with such loving reverence in *The Prelude* Wordsworth was put to school at Hawkshead, which then possessed one of the best grammar-schools of England, the famous school founded by Edwin Sandys, Archbishop of York, in the time of Queen Elizabeth. "The schoolmaster and the usher were to teach 'all such good authors which do contain precepts of virtue and good literature for the better education of youth, and shall once

---

[1] *Tintern Abbey*, 76—83.
[2] *The Prelude* I, 271—302.

every week at least instruct and examine the scholars in the principles of true religion, to the end that they may the better know and fear God.'" [1] Thanks to its liberal system of education the pupils of Hawkshead Grammar School were free to rove to their heart's content over the fields and the hills of the beautiful lake-district. We have seen in *Tintern Abbey* with what "dizzy joys" and "aching raptures" Wordsworth imbibed the mighty life of nature. About this phase in his nature-feeling he also speaks in *The Prelude*. Here he says that he was never more happy than when he and his friends returned home from their rambles

"Feverish with weary joints and beating minds." [2]

But even in this tempestuous time of physical delight he owed to nature "moods of subtler origin," [3] joys of an "intellectual charm." [4]

After this period of bodily enjoyment in nature there came a time, when things seen led to things unseen, a time, when he was seized by the soul of things, which, with a gigantic force, held him in its grasp, so strongly "that" he says

"bodily eyes
Were utterly forgotten, and what I saw
Appeared like something in myself, a dream,
A prospect in the mind." [5]

The "presences of nature in the sky and on the earth," "the visions of the hills" and "souls of lonely places" [6] were daily around the boy Wordsworth. In a trance, in a state of spiritual illumination, he beheld the world. He experienced the purifying, the ennobling influence of that which endures for ever.

"Mine was it in the fields both day and night,
And by the waters, all the summer long." [7]

---

[1] Eric Robertson, *Wordsworthshire*, p. 66.
[2] *The Prelude* II, 18.
[3] *Ibid.* I, 549.
[4] *Ibid.*, 553.
[5] *Ibid.* II, 348—352.
[6] *Ibid.* I, 463—466.
[7] *Ibid.*, 423—425.

What he possessed of spiritual treasures he owed to "the Wisdom and Spirit of the universe, the Soul that is the eternity of thought, that gives to forms and images a breath and everlasting motion." [1]

What incidents contributed towards producing this mystic fusion of his soul with the spirit of God in nature, Wordsworth tells us in *The Prelude* in some very striking and powerful passages. One night, when he went with a party of boys to catch woodcocks on the open heights, he took a bird from a springe which had been set by one of the others. After this transgression he heard "low breathings coming after him,"

> "sounds
> Of undistinguishable motion, steps
> Almost as silent as the turf they trod." [2]

Here the spirit of nature lays her hand on him. He becomes dimly conscious of a hidden life stirring behind her outward appearance. Another time, when he went climbing the high rocks to see the raven's nest and hung "on a perilous crag, but ill sustained by knots of grass and small fissures in the slippery rock," he exclaims:

> "With what strange utterance did the loud dry wind
> Blow through my ear! the sky seemed not a sky
> Of earth — and with what motion moved the clouds!" [3]

Here the boy feels again the supernatural in nature, something beyond what is to be seen with the bodily eye. This feeling of spiritual depth hidden in the shows of the external world gradually increased in strength. An instance of its intensity is very suggestively described in the following passage.

One summer-evening the boy unmoored a boat on Esthwaite Lake. It was an act of disobedience. Moonlight lay upon the water.

> "far above
> Was nothing but the stars and the grey sky." [4]

---

[1] *The Prelude* I, 401—404.
[2] *Ibid.*, 323—326.
[3] *Ibid.*, 337—340.
[4] *Ibid.*, 371—373.

Then, as he was cleaving the water in the silence of the night, suddenly, from the mountain-ridge before him a huge peak rose up, "as if with voluntary power instinct," a peak standing out black and ominous against the starry sky. It grew in size, and towered between him and the stars. It was a terrifying thing and suddenly he turned his boat round and rowed back through the glamour of the night with trembling heart. In chastened mood he walked across the meadows to Hawkshead and for days that night's spectacle haunted him. The boy was troubled by a sense of the undetermined, the unknown. Nature was no longer a tangible reality to him, but he dimly felt a hidden, mysterious life moving in the depth of her being. He caught a vague glimpse of a Presence, strangely remote, yet near, watching his secret acts, piercing into the moral consciousness of his interior life.

Legouis characterizes these impressions of the boy Wordsworth very suggestively. ,,Il n'est rien de plus subtil et de plus universel à la fois, que ces impressions. Si Wordsworth a été seul à les exprimer, il est impossible d'imaginer une époque ou un lieu de monde dans lesquels elles n'aient pas été ressenties. Elles sont à ce point élémentaires qu'il semble que seulement dans l'enfance de l'humanité elles aient pu être éprouvées avec cette intensité et traduites avec cette fraîcheur. Elles ont dû êtres celles des premiers créateurs de mythes, c'est à dire des premiers hommes. C'est une divinité, invisible, mais distinctement entendue, dont les pas ont poursuivi l'écolier après la faute commise. C'est quelque Titan courroucé que ce mont vivant dont l'apparition soudaine l'épouvante." [1]

But nature also impressed gentler, tenderer feelings on the boy's mind. When after a boat-race one day he and his friends reached a lovely island in the lake, the conqueror and the conquered were happy alike, because of the beauty of their surroundings. Envy was lost in the sight of the loveliness around them. Thus "the pride of strength was tempered," and he learnt the "self-sufficing power of solitude." Another time they visited the ruins of an ancient abbey in a lovely, secluded valley, and there, in the sweet peace of their surroundings, they heard a wren sing.

---

[1] Emile Legouis, *La Jeunesse de William Wordsworth*, p. 46.

> "So sweetly 'mid the gloom the invisible bird
> Sang to herself, that there I could have made
> My dwelling-place, and lived for ever there
> To hear such music." [1]

It seems so very simple, but how suggestive it is of mystical feeling. What a world of mystical emotion aroused by nature is enshrined in this "invisible," in the bird "singing to herself," in the wish of the poet to be "for ever" charmed by this heavenly melody. He loved the sun, not as the source and preserver of life, but because he had seen him lay his beauty on the morning hills." [2] One evening, when he returned home in his pinnace across the dark lake of Windermere, the sweet music of a flute sounded over the water. "Oh then," he says,

> "the calm
> And dead still water lay upon my mind
> Even with a weight of pleasure, and the sky,
> Never before so beautiful, sank down
> Into my heart, and held me like a dream!" [3]

These experiences were the prelude to the complete initiation into Reality which I referred to in the discussion of *Tintern Abbey*.

When afterwards Wordsworth was an undergraduate at Cambridge Nature upbore him amidst uncongenial surroundings. In a spirit of "religious love" he walked with her. She led him into the sanctuary of his heart, where God's voice was heard.

> "I was mounting now
> To such community with highest truth —
> A track pursuing, not untrod before,
> From strict analogies by thought supplied
> Or consciousness not to be subdued.
> To every natural form, rock, fruit, or flower,
> Even the loose stones that cover the highway,
> I gave a moral life: I saw them feel,
> Or linked them to some feeling: the great mass
> Lay bedded in a quickening soul, and all
> That I beheld respired with inward meaning.

---

[1] *The Prelude* II, 125—128.
[2] *Ibid.*, 183.
[3] *Ibid.*, 170—175.

Add that whate'er of Terror or of Love
Or Beauty, Nature's daily face put on
From transitory passion, unto this
I was as sensitive as waters are
To the sky's influence in a kindred mood
Of passion; was obedient as a lute
That waits upon the touches of the wind.
Unknown, unthought of, yet I was most rich —
I had a world about me — 't was my own;
I made it, for it only lived to me,
And to the God who sees into the heart." [1]

"I looked for universal things; perused
The common countenance of earth and sky:
. . . .
I called on both to teach me what they might;
Or turning the mind in upon herself,
Pored, watched, expected, listened, spread my thoughts
And spread them with a wider creeping; felt
Incumbencies more awful, visitings
Of the Upholder of the tranquil soul,
That tolerates the indignities of Time,
And, from the centre of Eternity
All finite motions overruling, lives
In glory immutable." [2]

One incident of great religious importance is what happened during a summer-vacation passed at Hawkshead, when Wordsworth was an undergraduate at Cambridge. After a night, spent in frivolous enjoyment, he, returning home, beheld the glory of the dawning day. The sea lay laughing at a distance, the mountains shone bright as the clouds, dew glittered and vapours floated.

                              To the brim
My heart was full; I made no vows, but vows
Were then made for me; bond unknown to me
Was given, that I should be, else sinning greatly,
A dedicated Spirit. On I walked
In thankful blessedness, which yet survives." [3]

This incident is a clear example of how in the moment of

---

[1] *The Prelude* III, 122—143.
[2] *Ibid.*, 106—121.
[3] *Ibid.*, IV, 333—339.

supreme inspiration Wordsworth feels himself lost in the mysterious power of a Spirit which transcends his own, which descends to him, and in its unknown majesty leads him to the heights of its holiness. In a passage like this we see the great difference between Wordsworth's nature-poetry and for instance Shelley's. Nature does not bring Shelley to the awe-inspiring feeling of moral responsibility, she does bring Wordsworth to it; and Wordsworth's nature-poetry is unique for this. What moved in the inwardness of the young undergraduate's soul was what shone out clear to the poet of the 24th Psalm: "Who shall ascend unto the hill of the Lord? or who shall stand in His holy place? He that hath clean hands and a pure heart; who hath not lifted up his soul unto vanity, nor sworn deceitfully. He shall receive the blessing from the Lord, and righteousness from the God of his salvation."

In another summer-vacation he went with his friend Robert Jones to Switzerland. The mighty scenery of the Alps appealed strongly to the sense of infinity and eternity in him. The Eternal in Nature spoke to the Eternal in him.

When a peasant whom they met on their way told them that they had crossed the Simplon, so that they had to descend, whilst they had "hopes that pointed to the clouds," he had one of his rare revelations:

> "Imagination — here the Power so called
> Through sad incompetence of human speech,
> That awful Power rose from the mind's abyss
> Like an unfathered vapour that enwraps,
> At once, some lonely traveller. I was lost;
> Halted without an effort to break through;
> But to my conscious soul I now can say —
> 'I recognise thy glory:' in such strength
> Of usurpation, when the light of sense
> Goes out, but with a flash that has revealed
> The invisible world, doth greatness make abode,
> There harbours; whether we be young or old,
> Our destiny, our being's heart and home,
> Is with infinitude, and only there;
> With hope it is, hope that can never die,
> Effort, and expectation, and desire,
> And something evermore about to be." [1]

---

[1] *The Prelude* VI, 592—609.

The immeasurable heights of woods, the blasts of waterfalls, the raving stream, the black drizzling crags

> "Were all like workings of one mind, the features
> Of the same face, blossoms upon one tree;
> Characters of the great Apocalypse,
> The type and symbols of Eternity,
> Of first, and last, and midst, and without end." [1]

The Excursion, another long poem, which was intended to be part of the never-finished *Recluse*, of which *The Prelude* was to be the introduction, also contains some very fine passages illustrative of Wordsworth's nature-mysticism.

One of the characters, figuring in this poem, the wanderer, whom, to a great extent, we can identify with Wordsworth himself, growing up in an atmosphere of grave piety and "plain living," far from the noisy unrest of the world, in the midst of the virginal loneliness of nature, would have, in shadowy intuitions, a mystical apprehension of the intangible unknown. When a boy of six, returning, after school-time, to his distant home, in solitude, he often

> "saw the hills
> Grow larger in the darkness, all alone
> Beheld the stars come out above his head,
> And travelled through the wood, with no one near
> To whom he might confess the things he saw." [2]

He was so overpowered by emotion at the obscure life stirring around him, at the mysterious grandeur of the things he saw, that

> "they lay
> Upon his mind like substances, whose presence
> Perplexed the bodily sense.
> . . . .
> in the after-day
> Of boyhood, many an hour in caves forlorn,
> And mid the hollow depths of naked crags
> He sate, and even in their fixed lineaments
> Or from the power of a peculiar eye,

---

[1] *Ibid.*, 636—641.
[2] *The Excursion* I, 127—132.

> Or by creative feeling overborne,
> Or by predominance of thought oppressed,
> Even in their fixed and steady lineaments
> He traced an ebbing and a flowing mind,
> Expression ever varying!" [1]

We see from this that the vision of the boy-wanderer from the early beginning is more spiritual than that of the boy-Wordsworth. The mystic power of nature already seizes him in the lonely evening-walk, when his heart, brimful of emotion, has only its own solitude to commune with. In the last quotation the creative power of the imagination in spiritual nature-vision is strongly stressed, but in neither is reached the trance-like state, which we found so beautifully described in *Tintern Abbey*, the state, when "the body is laid asleep and we become a living soul, seeing into the life of things." This initiation into the highest Reality came afterwards, when the boy had grown up to youth, and sitting on the naked top of some bold headland, he beheld the sun

> "Rise up and bathe the world in light. He looked —
> Ocean and earth, the solid frame of earth
> And Ocean's liquid mass, in gladness lay
> Beneath him: — Far and wide the clouds were touched,
> And in their silent faces could he read
> Unutterable love. Sound needed none,
> Nor any voice of joy; his spirit drank
> The spectacle: sensation, soul and form,
> All melted into him; they swallowed up
> His animal being; in them did he live,
> And by them did he live; they were his life.
> In such access of mind, in such high hour
> Of visitation from the living God,
> Thought was not; in enjoyment it expired.
> No thanks he breathed, he proffered no request;
> Rapt into still communion that transcends
> The imperfect offices of prayer and praise,
> His mind was a thanksgiving to the power
> That made him; it was blessedness and love!" [2]

---

[1] *The Excursion* I, 137—162.
[2] *Ibid.*, 200—219.

In this mystical ecstasy he possessed by sight what in other moments he grasped by faith. He saw the world borne by love, he saw it breathe immortality.

> "Early had he learned
> To reverence the volume that displays
> The mystery, the life which cannot die;
> But in the mountains did he *feel* his faith.
> All things, responsive to the writing, there
> Breathed immortality, revolving life,
> And greatness still revolving; infinite:
> There littleness was not; the least of things
> Seemed infinite; and there his spirit shaped
> Her prospects, nor did he believe, — he saw." [1]

Harper almost denies Wordsworth the high place of a nature-mystic, when he says: "Whether Wordsworth would have subscribed to the statement that the external world is a symbol of the Infinite Idea I very much doubt. There were moments, when he said so but when he is most himself he is most content with nature as reality and not as symbol." [2] I think that the passages which I have quoted in the course of this essay, justify a deviation from Harper's conception. In corroboration of my opinion I quote Legouis: „L'évanouissement du monde matériel est pour le poète une vérité plus haute et plus sûre que les plus ingenieux édifices philosophiques élevés par l'entendement de l'homme. Se servir des sens uniquement pour dresser le catalogue des aspects et des sons de la nature avec l'espoir d'atteindre ainsi à la parfaite connaissance, c'est les employer à l'usage le moins precieux. Chaque sensation doit mettre et met en realité en contact non avec l'objet qui la fait naître, mais avec l'âme qui est cachée derrière, avec la verité absolue." [3]

In connection with Harper's statement that Wordsworth was most content with nature as reality, and not as symbol, I would observe, that Wordsworth has written many inspired nature-poems in which the mystic revelation of God is not the predominant

---

[1] *The Excursion* I, 223—233.
[2] George Mclean Harper, *William Wordsworth, his Life, Works and Influence* I, p. 4.
[3] Legouis, *La Jeunesse de William Wordsworth*, p. 468.

feature, but this does not alter my attitude. *The Prelude* and the first two books of *The Excursion* contain much of Wordsworth's nature-poetry from 1798—1805. The shorter poems on nature which he wrote during that period are all of them a repetition in various forms of the power of nature presiding over man and beast, as *Three years she grew, Hart-Leap-Well, The Cuckoo, The Daffodils*; or they are a pure description of external beauty, but then in the intensity of the feeling they also lead us to something beyond the surface, as for example the beautiful *Sonnet, composed upon Westminster-Bridge*. *Three years she grew* and *The Cuckoo* are the most mystical of the above-mentioned poems. Lucy is moulded by nature into the loveliness of her own delights. Hers is the

> "breathing balm,
> And hers the silence and the calm
> Of mute insensate things."

The cuckoo is to the poet no longer a bird, but an "invisible thing," "a voice," "a mystery," "a hope, a love still longed for, never seen," and listening to the wandering voice he begets again the time of his "golden youth," when the world was steeped in the visionary light of fairyland.

This poem is akin in spirit to the Ode on *Intimations of Immortality from Recollections of early Childhood*. It also gives expression to a feeling of loss in visionary power, which the advancing years of manhood entail. There came a time, when the gleam, the dreamlike glory which surrounded the child's life vanished, and the visionary intensity with which things revealed themselves to him in his youth, makes Wordsworth look upon the child as a being endowed with superior wisdom (also expressed in *The Prelude*) and this susceptibility for the things of the spirit may be owing to the fact that the child is nearer to God, in direct communion with whom it lived in a pre-natal existence. But the vision of eternity which haunted the child in the sights of nature can still radiate the poet's life with much of its former mystic gleam.

> "Though inland far we be,
> Our Souls have sight of that immortal sea
> Which brought us hither." [1]

---
[1] *Intimations of Immortality* etc., 166—169.

There is a change, the child's unconscious, instinctive joys are tempered by the reflections of the adult, who knows human suffering, who has "kept watch o'er man's mortality," [1] but the poet has gained what he did not possess at the time of instinctive youth, the power to read with thoughtful consciousness the sublime wisdom of nature.

> "Thanks to the human heart by which we live,
> Thanks to its tenderness, its joys, and fears,
> To me the meanest flower that blows can give
> Thoughts that do often lie too deep for tears." [2]

This poem stands at the end of a period in which Wordsworth's poetic genius was in full activity. He had given his finest nature-poetry to the world. What followed did not bear on the whole that stamp of peculiar inspiration and vitality, except an *Evening-Ode* (1818), in which the poet "once more brings home to us that sense of belonging at once to two worlds, which gives to human life so much of mysterious solemnity." [3] It ends with a pathetic allusion to the visionary gleam, the heavenly light that lay about him in his infancy:

> "Full early lost, and fruitlessly deplored;
> Which, at this moment, on my waking sight
> Appears to shine, by miracle restored;
> My soul, though yet confined to earth,
> Rejoices in a second birth!
> — 'T is past, the visionary splendour fades;
> And night approaches with her shades." [4]

In connection with the different phases in Wordsworth's nature-feeling, I draw attention to an article of Marian Mead, in which she says: "If anything is true of Wordsworth it is that in youth, as always, his physical vision was normally bound up with spiritual powers. In the apparent contradiction of the *Tintern Abbey* passage, where he speaks of nature being "secondary to his own pursuits and animal activities," the poet turned in memory to a

---

[1] *Intimations of Immortality* etc., 202.
[2] *Ibid.*, 204—207.
[3] Myers, *Wordsworth*, p. 22.
[4] *Composed upon an Evening of extraordinary Splendour and Beauty*, 74—80.

phase in which, though thought and feeling were present, they were not distinct to consciousness from the visual impression, which in its ardour and fine careless rapture appeared all in all." [1] She adduces as a coroboration of her statement his exclamation: "What visionary powers of eye and soul in youth were mine." We might add among other proofs of the truth of her opinion:

> "I had known
> Too forcibly, too early in my life,
> Visitings of imaginative power
> For this (the predominance of the eye over the mind) to last." [2]

Hitherto Wordsworth has told us how he has been moulded and fashioned by nature, now we shall see that there was a mutual exchange of inspiring force between nature and himself. He revealed the "viewless agencies" of nature, and nature revealed him to himself. His keen sensibility felt nature as energetic life, his creative imagination heard in the sounds of the storm "the ghostly language of the ancient earth," "an auxiliar light" came from his mind "which on the setting sun bestowed new splendour." [3] And "the midnight storm grew darker in the presence of his eye." The moods of shadowy exultation which nature awakes in him are the life of his very soul, which finds again in them the essence of its being. The rapturous delight nature gave him was due to the mould of his inner self. Nature could not have revealed herself to him, if her spirit had not been his, if its creative energy had not inspired with life what his eye saw and his ear heard.

> "Coercing all things into sympathy,
> To unorganic natures were transferred
> My own enjoyments." [4]

---

[1] Marian Mead, *Wordsworth's Eye*, Publications of the Modern Language Associations XXXIV, p. 202.
[2] *The Prelude* XII, 201—204.
[3] *Ibid.* II, 369—370.
[4] *Ibid.*, 390—392.

Because his feeling was so subtle, his soul so deep, he could measure the depth of life, he could feel with bliss ineffable

> "the sentiment of Being spread
> O'er all that moves and all that seemeth still;
> O'er all that, lost beyond the reach of thought
> And human knowledge, to the human eye
> Invisible, yet liveth to the heart.
> . . . .
> Wonder not
> If high the transport, great the joy I felt
> Communing in this sort through earth and heaven
> With every form of creature, as it looked
> Towards the Uncreated with a countenance
> Of adoration, with an eye of love.
> One song they sang, and it was audible,
> Most audible, then, when the fleshly ear,
> O'ercome by humblest prelude of that strain,
> Forgot her functions, and slept undisturbed." [1]

These lines are expressive of one of Wordsworth's very high stretches of mystical imagination. Coleridge understood the secret of his friend's vision as an inner light transfusing the exterior world into its likeness.

> "Power streamed from thee, and thy soul received
> The light reflected as a light bestowed." [2]

He measured the depth of that mind, which, stirred by "vital breathings, secret as the soul of vernal growth," often quickens the heart into thoughts "all too deep for words."

Coleridge expresses his views as to the relation between nature and man's mind in *Dejection*, that very fine poem, in which the whole moving tragedy of his shattered life is laid bare.

> "we receive but what we give
> And in our life alone does nature live.
> . . . .
> Ah! from the soul itself must issue forth
> A light, a glory, a fair luminous cloud
> Enveloping the Earth." [3]

---

[1] *The Prelude* II, 401—406, 409—419.
[2] Coleridge, *To William Wordsworth*, 18—20.
[3] *Dejection*, 47—49, 53—55.

He experiences that nature, notwithstanding her outward beauty, may fail to rouse man to spiritual raptures. He gazes on the evening-sky in its peculiar tint of yellow green, he observes the motion of the clouds and exclaims:

> "I see them all so excellently fair,
> I see, not feel, how beautiful they are!" [1]

This creative imagination is described by Wordsworth as a "plastic power," which abode with him,

> "a forming hand, at times
> Rebellious, acting in a devious mood;
> A local spirit of his own, at war
> With general tendency, but, for the most,
> Subservient strictly to external things
> With which it communed." [2]

In another place in *The Prelude* he says:

> "The mind is lord and master, outward sense
> The obedient servant of her will." [3]

The mind "feeds upon infinity", it

> "broods over the dark abyss, intent to hear
> Its voices issuing forth to silent light
> In one continuous stream." [4]

The spiritual love by which he feels the world upborne

> acts not nor can exist
> "Without Imagination, which, in truth,
> Is but another name for absolute power
> And clearest insight, amplitude of mind,
> And Reason in her most exalted mood." [5]

From her, which he calls feeling intellect, intellectual love, he drew

> "Faith in life endless, the sustaining thought
> Of human Being, Eternity and God." [6]

---

[1] *Dejection*, 37—39.
[2] *The Prelude* II, 362—368.
[3] *Ibid.* XII, 222—224.
[4] *Ibid.* XIV, 71—84.
[5] *Ibid.*, 188—192.
[6] *Ibid.*, 204—206.

And at the end of *The Prelude*, when he has traced the nature of his vision to its very source he declares that

>"the mind of man becomes
>A thousand times more beautiful than the earth
>On which he dwells, above this frame of things
>(Which, 'mid all revolution in the hopes
>And fears of men, doth still remain unchanged)
>In beauty exalted, as it is itself
>Of quality and fabric more divine." [1]

Harper's opinion is that *The Prelude*, especially the last three books of it, which were finished in 1805, and which set forth this theory of the mutual relation between the mind and nature, renounce the faith expressed in *Tintern Abbey*. At the time he wrote that poem, "he would have considered it blasphemy to speak of the mind of man as overleaping nature." [2] I cannot agree with Harper. On the contrary rather do I find in *The Prelude* a maturing of the belief expressed in *Tintern Abbey*, or rather a more conscious expression of it. Through the intensity of sentiment with which he felt nature, he was led to his belief in the mind's power. She was to him the instrument through which the songs of the universe found expression. As I already observed, he never dissociated the external world from the human heart, not even in *Tintern Abbey*, and this is one of the very sources of his strength. [3] The "sensations sweet, felt in the blood and felt along the heart," of which he speaks in *Tintern Abbey*, are the result of this indissoluble relation between the mind and nature. In the same poem he speaks of "the mighty world of eye and ear, both what they half create and what perceive." [4] Besides, we must not forget that he spoke of the "plastic power" of the imagination already being his, when he was a school-boy at Hawkshead. [5]

We have seen that in Wordsworth's mysticism the luminative

---

[1] *The Prelude* XIV, 448—454.
[2] Harper, *Wordsworth*, etc. II, 148.
[3] See Marian Mead, *Wordsworth's Eye*, Publications of the Modern Language Association XXXIV, p. 202.
[4] *Tintern Abbey*, 106.
[5] *The Prelude* II, 362.

and the unitive stage is to be observed, we can also trace a period of purgation. [1]

"The mystic vision was not attained by him any more than by others without deliberate renunciation. He lays great stress upon this and yet it is a point in his teaching sometimes overlooked. He insists repeatedly on the fact that before any one can taste of these joys of the spirit, he must be purified, disciplined, self controlled." [2]

"The ascetic element in Wordsworth's ethics should by no means be forgotten by those who envy his brave and unruffled outlook upon life. As Hutton says excellently, (*Essays*, p. 81) 'there is volition and self-government in every line of his poetry, and his best thoughts come from the steady resistance he opposes to the ebb and flow of ordinary desires and regrets. He contests the ground inch by inch with all despondent and indolent humours, and often, too, with movements of inconsiderate and wasteful joy — turning defeat into victory, and victory into defeat." [3]

It is only the pure in heart that shall see God. Coleridge expresses it in his Ode on *Dejection*

> "joy was never given,
> Save to the pure, and in their purest hour." [4]

Wordsworth did not waste the powers of his imagination

> "as in the wordling's mind,
> On fickle pleasures, and superfluous cares,
> And trivial ostentation." [5]

His mind was focussed on such objects as

> "excite
> No morbid passions, no disquietude,
> No vengeance and no hatred."

He can testify that

> whatsoever falls my better mind
> Revolving with the accidents of life,

[1] See note 2, p. 4.
[2] Caroline Spurgeon, *Mysticism in English Literature*, p. 64.
[3] Inge, *Christian Mysticism*, p. 308.
[4] Coleridge, *Dejection*, 64—66.
[5] *The Excursion* IV, 820—822.

> May have sustained, that, howsoe'er misled,
> Never did I, in quest of right and wrong,
> Tamper with conscience from a private aim;
> Nor was in any public hope the dupe
> Of selfish passions, nor did ever yield
> Wilfully to mean cares or low pursuits,
> But shrunk with apprehensive jealousy
> From every combination which might aid
> The tendency, too potent in itself,
> Of use and custom to bow down the soul
> Under a growing weight of vulgar sense,
> And substitute a universe of death
> For that which moves with light and life informed,
> Actual, divine and true." [1]

And this purity of heart, this being stripped of all extraneous ornaments of life, this emptiness of the world, which may receive the fullness of God, is again closely related to the communion with nature; there is a reciprocal action between them, the cleansed mind is able to receive the wisdom of nature, and the wisdom of nature is felt in an enhanced moral consciousness. This is very beautifully expressed in a passage in *The Prelude* which has already been referred to, when the poet, walking round the lake which was so redolent of the sweet remembrances of his childhood felt in the nakedness of his soul, which had gently put off her veil as in the presence of his God. The description that follows of this marvellous walk with God proves clearly, how in this highest experience nature is dissolved and the Divine Presence is felt in an increased moral vitality.

> "Of that external scene which round me lay,
> Little, in this abstraction, did I see;
> Remembered less; but I had inward hopes
> And swellings of the spirit, was rapt and soothed,
> Conversed with promises, had glimmering views
> How life pervades the undecaying mind;
> How the immortal soul with God-like power
> Informs, creates, and thaws the deepest sleep
> That time can lay upon her; how on earth
> Man, if he do but live within the light
> Of high endeavours, daily spreads abroad
> His being armed with strength that cannot fail." [2]

---

[1] *The Prelude* XIV, 147—162.
[2] *Ibid.* IV, 159—172.

NATURE   127

We find in Wordsworth's poetry again and again testimonies of the inspiring power of solitude, which is the atmosphere in which the pure life can be lived, solitude, always as an inner detachment from extraneous, inessential pursuits of life, and mostly combined with an avoidance of the crowds of great cities, noisy companies, distracting environment. This is the essential attitude of mind of all mystics. In the middle-ages there were many who retired into the solitude of the cloister, St. Francis of Assisi and his followers took Lady Poverty for their bride and went through the land in absolute destitution of worldly possessions. The same principle is at the root of their action. They have all felt, have found the truth that the road to God leads along the renunciation of what gratifies the surface-mind, the truth of Christ's paradox: "Who shall lose his life shall find it."

The following quotations all testify to "the bliss of solitude."

"Full oft the quiet and exalted thoughts
Of loneliness gave way to empty noise
And superficial pastimes." [1]

"Hitherto I had stood
In my own mind remote from social life,
(At least from what we commonly so name,)
Like a lone shepherd on a promontory
Who lacking occupation looks far forth
Into the boundless sea, and rather makes
Than finds what he beholds." [2]

There was an inner falling of — a swarm
Of heady schemes jostling each other, gawds
And feast and dance, and public revelry,
And sports and games (too grateful in themselves,
Yet in themselves less grateful, I believe,
Than as they were a badge glossy and fresh
Of manliness and freedom) all conspired
To lure my mind from firm habitual quest
Of feeding pleasures, to depress the zeal
And damp those yearnings which had once been mine —

---

[1] *The Prelude* III, 207—209.
[2] *Ibid.*, 510—516.

A wild unworldly-minded youth, given up
To his own eager thoughts." [1]

"It seemed the very garments that I wore
Preyed on my strength and stopped the quiet stream
Of self-forgetfulness." [2]

When from our better selves we have too long
Been parted by the hurrying world, and droop,
Sick of its business, of its pleasures tired,
How gracious, how benign, is Solitude." [3]

"And — now convinced at heart
How little those formalities, to which
With overweening trust alone we give
The name of Education, have to do
With real feeling and just sense; how vain
A correspondence with the talking world
Proves to the most." [4]

We feel in this modern poet a similar spirit living as in the mediaeval monk who in the solitude of his cloister-cell found his fullness of life and bequeathed to his fellow-men on the pilgrim's road in his "golden booklet" the treasure which he found shining in the holy loneliness of his heart.

Houd u, zooveel gij kunt, verre van het druk gewoel der menschen,
want het bespreken van wereldsche zaken is een groot beletsel,
ook al geschiedt het met een zuivere bedoeling.
Want zoo ras worden wij door ijdelheid besmet en omstrikt.
Ik wenschte wel dat ik meer gezwegen had,
en dat ik niet onder de menschen geweest ware." [5]

"Zoek een gelegenen tijd om met u zelven alleen te zijn,
en overdenk menigwerf de weldaden van God.

Zoo gij u onttrekken wilt aan noodelooze gesprekken,
aan een ijdel gaan van den een tot den ander,

---

[1] *The Prelude* IV, 278—291.
[2] *Ibid.*, 925—297.
[3] *Ibid.*, 354—358.
[4] *Ibid.* XIII, 168—174.
[5] Thomas à Kempis, *De Navolging van Christus*, vertaling van Dr. Is. v. Dijk, hoofdstuk 10.

ook aan het opvangen van allerlei nieuws en gerucht, zult gij overvloedigen en bekwamen tijd vinden om u te wijden aan vrome overdenkingen."

"Iemand heeft eens gezegd:
‚Zoo dikwijls ik onder menschen geweest ben, ben ik altijd minder thuis gekomen!' "

"Zoo wie dan begeert tot een innerlijk en geestelijk leven te komen, hij moet, met Jezus, de schare ontwijken." [1]

In Wordsworth's attitude towards the world and eternity we also recognize Eckhart's "Abgeschiedenheit," which is considered by him to be the highest virtue, because it is receptive of God. "Gottes natürliche, eigenste Stätte ist Einheit und Lauterkeit; die aber beruhen auf Abgeschiedenheit. Darum kann Gott nicht umhin, einem abgeschiedenen Herzen sich selber zu geben." [2]

Inge says of Wordsworth: "In aloofness and loneliness of mind he is exceeded by no mystic of the cloisters." [3]

My survey of Wordsworth's nature-poetry shows clearly Irving Babbit's statement that one of the reasons why pantheistic revery was so popular in the romantic period is that it seems to offer a painless substitute for genuine spiritual effort, when applied to Wordsworth, to be decidedly wide of the mark. [4]

By nature a mystic, he tried in noble endeavour, to fulfil the high destiny of his calling.

---

[1] Thomas à Kempis, *De Navolging van Christus*, hoofdstuk 20.
[2] Eckhart, *Schriften und Predigten* I, p. 57. See p. 107.
[3] Inge, *Christian Mysticism*, p. 307.
[4] Irving Babbitt, *Rousseau and Romanticism*, p. 286.

Chapter XII

THE CHILD

Like Blake Wordsworth saw the child clothed in a heavenly radiance. He pierced through the child's soul into the abyss of God's being, catching through its light glimpses of His clarity, groping through its transparency towards the realms of supernal Wisdom. Wordsworth's vision of the child was born of the luminous remembrance of his own childhood among the happy hills and serene lakes of the land of his birth. The emotion which moved the boy Wordsworth, as the wonders of nature unrolled themselves before his enraptured gaze, clung as a blessed remembrance to the man and was afterwards felt by maturer experience as the intuitive adumbration of the supersensual world. In the famous words: "The child is father of the man," which he put as motto over the famous Ode on *Intimations of Immortality*, he paid reverent tribute to the divine revelations of his infancy.

As the child Wordworth's predominating emotion was born of nature's inspiring force, it follows that his nature-poetry is very closely interwoven with his songs on children, and as his vision of childhood was rooted in his own experience, we shall find much of it embodied in his autobiographical poem, *The Prelude*, which is a glorification both of nature and of the child. So much of what I said in the discussion of Wordsworth's nature-mysticism I might repeat here.

The grand propelling force of Wordsworth's child is nature, the inscrutable Mystery, which fills the soul with awe and wonder, the great Life, which is the mirror of Eternity. Reference has been made to the fact that for Wordsworth the visionary glory in which the child's life was steeped faded with advancing years, and the child's greater intensity of intuitive sensibility led him into a belief of a pre-natal existence of the soul in the bosom of Eternity.

> Our childhood sits,
> Our simple childhood, sits upon a throne
> That hath more power than all the elements.
> I guess not what this tells of Being past,
> Nor what it augurs of the life to come;
> But so it is, and, in that dubious hour,
> That twilight when we first begin to see
> This dawning earth, to recognise, expect,
> And, in the long probation that ensues,
> The time of trial, ere we learn to live
> In reconcilement with our stinted powers;
> To endure this state of meagre vassalage,
> Unwilling to forego, confess, submit,
> Uneasy and unsettled, yoke-fellows
> To custom, mettlesome, and not yet tamed
> And humbled down; — oh! then we feel, we feel,
> We know where we have friends." [1]

In another place in *The Prelude* he exclaims:

> "O Heavens! how awful is the might of souls,
> And what they do within themselves while yet
> The yoke of earth is new to them, the world
> Nothing but a wild field where they were sown."

The reminiscence of a pre-natal existence glimmers through these lines, but in the famous Ode on *Intimations of Immortality from Recollections of early Childhood* it is expressed definitely. When nature's beauties could no longer stir in the poet those deep emotions which had moved the heart of the child, there was born of the memory of lost glory the belief in a Heavenly Home, where the soul lived in the bosom of God, before the bonds of the body enclosed it. The child, being nearer to its divine origin than the grown-up man, has a purer vision of reality, hence the supernal atmosphere in which its life is steeped.

Solemnly like a hymn in its mighty rhythm, the music that sings of man's Celestial Source and Destiny comes surging on:

[1] *The Prelude* V, 507—524.
[2] *Ibid.* III, 177—181.

> "Our birth is but a sleep and a forgetting:
> The Soul that rises with us, our life's Star,
>   Hath had elsewhere its setting,
>   And cometh from afar:
>   Not in entire forgetfulness,
>   And not in utter nakedness,
> But trailing clouds of glory do we come
>   From God, who is our home:
> Heaven lies about us in our infancy!
> Shades of the prison-house begin to close
>   Upon the growing Boy,
> But He beholds the light, and whence it flows,
>   He sees it in his joy;
> The Youth, who daily farther from the east
>   Must travel, still is Nature's Priest,
>   And by the vision splendid
>   Is on his way attended;
> At length the Man perceives it die away,
> And fade into the light of common day." [1]

Here we have Wordsworth at his highest. With him the poet and the mystic go often hand in hand. True inspiration with him as a rule opens the gates of mystic vision, which in its purest aspect is clear and shining, and the form in which the spirit is clothed seems to rise then of its own accord like an exhalation from the depth of pure Being.

Wordsworth does not exalt the child to its high place, because of the happy liberty of its life, because of its simple faith and hopeful expectation, the grace and charm of its unconscious spontaneity and pure enjoyment, but he worships in the child's sanctuary, because of the intensity of its intuition, by which it dives into the Mystery of Being, is illumined by the Supernal Light and receives the sacrament of Eternal Life.

He addresses the child as the "best Philosopher," a "mighty Prophet," "Seer blest," an "Eye among the blind,"

> "That, deaf and silent, read'st the eternal deep,
> Haunted for ever by the eternal mind."
> . . . .
>   O joy! that in our embers
>   Is something that doth live,
>   That nature yet remembers
>   What was so fugitive!

---
[1] *Intimations of Immortality* V.

> The thought of our past years in me doth breed
> Perpetual benediction: not indeed
> For that which is most worthy to be blest;
> Delight and liberty, the simple creed
> Of Childhood, whether busy or at rest,
> With new-fledged hope still fluttering in his breast: —
>   Not for these I raise
>   The song of thanks and praise;
>   But for those obstinate questionings
>   Of sense and outward things,
>   Fallings from us, vanishings;
>   Blank misgivings of a Creature
> Moving about in worlds not realised,
> High instincts before which our mortal Nature
> Did tremble like a guilty thing surprised:
>   But for those first affections,
>   Those shadowy recollections,
>   Which, be they what they may,
> Are yet the fountain-light of all our day,
> Are yet a master-light of all our seeing;
>   Uphold us, cherish and have power to make
> Our noisy years seem moments in the being
> Of the eternal Silence: truths that wake,
>   To perish never:
> Which neither listlessness, nor mad endeavour,
>   Nor Man, nor Boy,
> Nor all that is at enmity with joy,
> Can utterly abolish or destroy!
>   Hence in a season of calm weather
>   Though inland far we be,
> Our Souls have sight of that immortal sea
>   Which brought us hither,
>   Can in a moment travel thither,
> And see the Children sport upon the shore,
> And hear the mighty waters rolling evermore." [1]

So we see that the child's transports of mystical emotion continue to inspire the man; something of the light of his infancy still shines with a transcendental gleam over the days of his manhood. Therefore he adores the child as the mediator between the world of Reality and himself.

"Our noisy years moments in the being of the eternal Silence;" this is the expression of the purely mystic state, the sinking of the

[1] *Intimations of Immortality* VIII, 113—115, IX.

individual into the Absolute, the dissolving of all earthly ties in the abyss of the Uncreated. About what "those obstinate questionings of sense and outward things, fallings from us, vanishings," which are his descent into the "abyss of idealism," are, Wordsworth spoke to some acquaintances. The Reverend Robert Perceval Graves of Windermere in a letter written in 1850 to Mr. Hawes Turner, editor of *Selections from Wordsworth*, says: "I remember Mr. Wordsworth saying, that at a particular stage of his mental progress, he used to be frequently so rapt into an unreal transcendental world of ideas that the external world seemed no longer to exist in relation to him, and he *had to reconvince himself of its existence by clasping a tree, or something that happened to be near him.*"[1] In a letter by Professor Bonamy Price to Mr. Turner we find the same idea expressed. He says: "You will be glad, I am sure, to receive an interpretation, which chance enabled me to obtain from Wordworth himself of a passage in the immortal 'Ode on Immortality.'.... It happened one day that the poet, my wife, and I were taking a walk together by the side of Rydal Water. We were then by the sycamores under Nab Scar. The aged poet was in a most genial mood, and it suddenly occurred to me that I might, without unwarrantable presumption, seize the golden opportunity thus offered, and ask him to explain these mysterious words. So I addressed him with an apology, and begged him to explain, what my own feeble mother-wit was unable to unravel, and for which I had in vain sought the assistance of others, what were those 'fallings from us, vanishings', for which, above all other things, he gave God thanks. The venerable old man raised his aged form erect, he was walking in the middle, and passed across me to a five-barred gate in the wall which bounded the road on the side of the lake. He clenched the top bar firmly with his right hand, pushed strongly against it, and then uttered these ever-memorable words: 'There was a time in my life when I had to push against something that resisted, to be sure that there was anything outside of me. I was sure of my own mind; everything else fell away and vanished into thought.' Thought, he was sure

---

[1] *Poems*, edited by William Knight, VIII, 201 n., quoted by E. Hershey Sneath in *Wordsworth, Poet of Nature and Poet of Man*, p. 211.

This idea is also expressed in a *Fenwick note, Poems*, Knight, VIII, 189 n., quoted by Sneath in *Wordsworth, etc.*, p. 214.

of; matter for him, at the moment, was an unreality — nothing but a thought. Such natural spontaneous idealism has probably never been felt by any other man." [1]

So we see how overpoweringly the spiritual world took hold of him, how in mystical trance he was lost to the earth and breathed in worlds "to which the heaven of heavens is but a veil." [2]

Thus much about the autobiographical element in Wordsworth's poetry on childhood. He has also sung about other children than himself. The little ones whom he met in his rambles through the field or those who brightened his home or that of his friends, occupied an important place in his affections and often illumined him with flashes of insight lying beyond the ken of the grown-up man. One of the best-known among the children's songs is *We are Seven*. The cottage-girl whom the poet meets on the road is seen in a mystic light. A halo of freshness, purity, simplicity and innocence radiates round her. She breathes the spirit of the fields and the woods. All the spontaneous life of nature thrills in the youth of her graceful limbs, shines in the fairness of her eyes. Her beauty is a gladdening presence and the poet feels fascinated by the natural charm of her being. And this simple child proves, in her very simplicity, to be an initiate into the mystery of life and death. She is illumined by an inner light, which leads her to the regions of mystic knowledge, where death and separation do not exist.

On the poet's reiterated question how many they are at home, she persists in answering that they are seven, thus including her little sister and brother, who are dead and who rest in the churchyard beside the little cottage, where she lives with her mother.

> " 'Sisters and brothers, little maid,
> How many may you be?'
> 'How many? Seven in all,' she said,
> And wondering looked at me.
>
> 'And where are they? I pray you tell.'
> She answered, 'Seven are we;
> And two of us at Conway dwell,
> And two are gone to sea.

---

[1] *Poetical Works*, Knight, VIII, 201—202 n., quoted by Sneath in *Wordsworth, etc.*, p. 212.
[2] *The Excursion*, Introduction, 30.

'Two of us in the church-yard lie,
My sister and my brother,
And, in the church-yard cottage, I
Dwell near them with my mother.'

'You say that two at Conway dwell,
And two are gone to sea,
Yet ye are seven! I pray you tell,
Sweet Maid, how this may be.'

Then did the little Maid reply,
'Seven boys and girls are we;
Two of us in the churchyard lie,
Beneath the church-yard tree.'

'You run about, my little Maid,
Your limbs they are alive;
If two are in the Church-yard laid,
Then ye are only five.' "

With exquisite simplicity and touching tenderness, in a description haunted by a superterrestrial spirit of quiet and peace, the little girl proceeds to tell him how she lives in daily intercourse with those who have been laid asleep beneath the green grass in the shade of the churchyard tree.

" 'Their graves are green, they may be seen,'
The little Maid replied.
'Twelve steps or more from my mother's door,
And they are side by side.

'My stockings there I often knit,
My kerchief there I hem,
And there upon the ground I sit,
And sing a song to them.

'And often after sun-set, Sir,
When it is light and fair,
I take my little porringer,
And eat my supper there.' "

And she continues to tell him about the illness and subsequent death of her brother and sister in a most affecting acceptance of things, without complaint, without questioning about the mystery of suffering and death, which does not exist in the pure clarity of her mind.

> " 'The first that died was sister Jane;
> In bed she moaning lay,
> Till God released her of her pain;
> And then she went away.'
>
> 'So in the church-yard she was laid,
> And, when the grass was dry,
> Together round her grave we played,
> My brother John and I.
>
> 'And when the ground was white with snow,
> And I could run and slide,
> My brother John was forced to go,
> And he lies by her side.' "

At this the poet once more asks the question: "How many are you then?" to which the little Maid replies:

> " 'O Master, we are seven.'
>
> 'But they are dead, those two are dead!
> Their spirits are in heaven!'
> 'Twas throwing words away; for still
> The little Maid would have her will,
> And said, 'Nay, we are seven!' "

To many the girl's notion of her dead sister and brother still being part of the family, is due to her animal vivacity which cannot conceive of a ceasing of life, a conception which is strengthened by the opening stanza:[1]

> "A simple Child,
> That lightly draws its breath,
> And feels its life in every limb,
> What should it know of death?"

I have shown in my interpretation of the poem that according to my conception it is due to a deeper experience. I share this belief with Bradley, who in a note to his essay on Wordsworth [2] explains from internal and external evidence the girl's pertinacity in ignoring the fact of death, to arise from an intuitive fore-feeling

---
[1] I draw attention to the fact that it was written by Coleridge.
[2] Bradley, *Oxford Lectures*, p. 146.

of immortality. Thus it is allied to the great Ode. A contemporary of Wordworth, De Quincey, already hints at this conception.[1]

Beatty, who explains Wordworth's poetry in the light of associationism disagrees with Bradley's conception. "This is a thoroughly associationistic poem," he says, "for the child's insensibility to death is accounted for by the life that is in her limbs. She has not yet received even such an elementary lesson in feeling for others as is given by the expiring candle in the *Letter* to 'Mathetes.' She has the utter self-concentration and insensibility of the child. Professor A. C. Bradley argues that the child has not the idea of death because she has a feeling for immortality. But the idea of immortality is just as far removed from the child as is the fear of death; that is, immortality as a judgment and applicable to others. .... The child has no general notion of death, as its mind is not sufficiently developed to entertain such a general judgment. But the germs are there, and, in accordance with associationistic principles these will develop into a judgment which will include not only the idea of death but the belief in immortality. To connect such ideas as death and immortality in a single idea is beyond the child, and all children would make an answer similar to that of the little maid. Therefore, despite Professor Bradley's doubts, the thought of the poem is expressed in the opening stanza, if we give it the proper Wordsworthian interpretation, in terms of associationism."[2]

I agree with Beatty in so far that a child would not philosophize on death and immortality, but the absence of philosophy in the child's belief is the key to its mysticism. When we enter into the spirit of the poem we find more than the girl's feeling of animal vivacity and absolute insensibility for others in the self-concentration of its undeveloped mind. Our mystic consciousness is stirred when we read about the little girl's daily intercourse with those who have departed to the Unseen Land.

" 'My stockings there I often knit,
My kerchief there I hem;

---

[1] De Quincey, *Recollections of the Lakes and the Lake-poets.*
[2] Arthur Beatty, *William Wordsworth, his Doctrine and Art in their historical Relations*, pp. 186, 187, 188.

> And there upon the ground I sit,
> And sing a song to them.
>
> 'And often after sun-set, Sir,
> When it is light and fair,
> I take my little porringer,
> And eat my supper there.' "

In these lines there is an unearthly quiet, which breathes the mute solemnity, the unruffled peace of death. This is the child's dream, which to the child is reality, to the man aspiration. And the reality of the dream is the child's unconsciousness of dreaming it. And the adult may gain in tears and sobs the faith which heals the grief of bereavement, he may have a vision of the mystic Land where death is life and life death, yet the dream of the child will remain a lost Paradise to him and Wordsworth always felt this and deplored it. The undertone which is heard in the *Ode to Immortality* is also, though less definitely, heard here.

Not less charming than the girl in *We are Seven* is the little boy in *Anecdote for Fathers*. Wordsworth is careful to describe him to us, like the cottage-girl as a pure child of nature, full of grace and sunshiny vivacity. The picture of the child and of nature singing and jubilant around it, is of an exquisite beauty, peculiarly Wordsworthian, pellucid, pure and simple.

> "I have a boy of five years old;
> His face is fair and fresh to see;
> His limbs are cast in beauty's mould,
> And dearly he loves me.
>
> One morn we strolled on our dry walk,
> Our quiet home all full in view,
> And held such intermitted talk
> As we are wont to do.
>
> My thoughts on former pleasures ran;
> I thought of Kilve's delightful shore,
> Our pleasant home when spring began,
> A long, long year before.
>
> A day it was when I could bear
> Some fond regrets to entertain;

With so much happiness to spare,
I could not feel a pain.

The green earth echoed to the feet
Of lambs that bounded through the glade,
From shade to sunshine, and as fleet
From sunshine back so shade.

Birds warbled round me — and each trace
Of inward sadness had its charm;
Kilve, thought I, was a favoured place,
And so is Liswyn farm.

My boy beside me tripped, so slim
And graceful in his rustic dress!
And, as we talked, I questioned him,
In very idleness."

And this child, free and joyous as the birds and the lambs in the field, does not like being importuned with the poet's meddlesome questioning and answers at random, simply to be rid of the trouble.

" 'Now tell me, had you rather be,'
I said and took him by the arm,
'On Kilve's smooth shore, by the green sea,
Or here at Liswyn farm?'

In careless mood he looked at me,
While still I held him by the arm.
And said, 'At Kilve I'd rather be
Than here at Liswyn farm.'

'Now, little Edward, say why so:
My little Edward, tell me why.' —
'I cannot tell, I do not know.' —
'Why, this is strange,' said I.

'For here are woods, hills, smooth and warm:
There surely must some reason be
Why you would change sweet Liswyn farm
For Kilve by the green sea.'

At this my boy hung down his head,
He blushed with shame, nor made reply;
And three times to the child I said,
'Why, Edward, tell me why?'

> His head he raised — there was in sight,
> It caught his eye, he saw it plain —
> Upon the house-top, glittering bright,
> A broad and gilded vane.
>
> Then did the boy his tongue unlock,
> And eased his mind with this reply:
> 'At Kilve there was no weather-cock;
> And that's the reason why.' "

Then suddenly it breaks in upon the poet what wisdom is enshrined in the careless liberty and impulsive gladness of the boy, who does not analyze and investigate, but who rejoices in the pure feeling of abundant life. And the poet ends with the exclamation

> "Oh dearest, dearest boy! my heart
> For better lore would seldom yearn,
> Could I but teach the hundredth part
> Of what from thee I learn."

A poem, breathing a somewhat different spirit, but yet one of Wordsworth's finest and most mystic songs on children is *To H(artley) C(oleridge), six years old*. His vision of the child is highly imaginative and mystic. It is seen by him as pure essence of life, ethereal, impalpable, vanishing at the soiling touch of earthly things. The child is addressed thus by the poet:

> "O Thou! whose fancies from afar are brought;
> Who of thy words dost make a mock apparel,
> And fittest to unutterable thought
> The breeze-like motion and the self-born carol;
> Thou faery voyager! that dost float
> In such clear water, that thy boat
> May rather seem
> To brood on air than on an earthly stream;
> Suspended in a stream as clear as sky,
> Where earth and heaven do make one imagery;
> O blessèd vision! happy child!
> Thou art so exquisitely wild,
> I think of thee with many fears
> For what may be thy lot in future years."

So fear for the future of this happy boy rises in the poet's heart. What, if life's grief comes to throw its shadow over his pure enjoyment?

But the poet immediately checks his uneasy thoughts. It is borne in upon him that the spirit of life as embodied in this child is eternal.

> "O too industrious folly!
> O vain and causeless melancholy!
> Nature will either end thee quite;
> Or, lengthening out thy season of delight,
> Preserve for thee, by individual right,
> A young lamb's heart among the full-grown flocks.
> What hast thou to do with sorrow,
> Or the injuries of to-morrow?
> Thou art a dew-drop, which the morn brings forth,
> Ill fitted to sustain unkindly shocks,
> Or to be trailed along the soiling earth;
> A gem that glitters while it lives,
> And no forewarning gives;
> But, at the touch of wrong, without a strife,
> Slips in a moment out of life."

And with this poem we shall take leave of Wordsworth's songs about children. Those which I have discussed are his most typical, and are representative of his mystic vision of the child.

The Pet-Lamb, for example, however sweetly beautiful, I could leave out of discussion, because in it the peculiar mystic note is not rung, unless we should call mysticism everything that moves the heart to an uncommon depth of emotion, unless we should call mysticism the poet's being haunted by the sweet melody of the charming girl, by the tender grace of her being, in such a way, as to lose almost his own identity in the glamour of her personality.

> "As homeward through the lane I went with lazy feet,
> This song to myself did I oftentimes repeat;
> And it seemed, as I retraced the ballad line by line,
> That but half of it was hers, and one half of it was *mine*.
>
> Again, and once again did I repeat the song;
> 'Nay,' said I, 'more than half to the damsel must belong,
> For she looked with such a look, and she spake with such a tone,
> That I almost received her heart into my own."

Coleridge says in *Biographia Literaria* [1] that one of the defects in Wordsworth's poetry is that it contains thoughts and images too great for the subject. Speaking of the Ode on *Intimations of Immortality* he says: "In what sense is a child of that age a Philosopher? In what sense is he declared to be for ever haunted by the Supreme Being? or so inspired as to deserve the splendid titles of a 'Mighty Prophet, a blessed Seer?' Children at this age give us no information of themselves; and at what time were we dipped in the Lethe, which has produced such utter oblivion of a state so godlike?"

Sometimes I am inclined to ask: "Cannot it be that he exalted the child too high, that he poured his own great poet-soul into the child's, that the glory in which his youth was seen by him was to a great extent a reflection of the light that enlightened his mind?" But then, when I think of the high-wrought ecstacy, the soaring imagination, the thrilling inspiration of the poetry that sings of his childhood, I feel that we are not justified in detracting anything from the value of the spiritual debt which Wordsworth declared he owed to the revelations that illumined the happy years of his infancy.

---

[1] Coleridge, *Biographia Literaria*, Every man's library, p. 246.

Chapter XIII

MAN

Wordsworth's mysticism of man is again closely related to that of nature. Man, being a part of nature, is not to be separated from her. Wordsworth's sensitive heart thrilled in mystical emotion to all utterances of life, in whatever form revealed. The interrelation of created things was grasped in the depth of his being. It was nature, in whom the wonder of life was first revealed to him, and she gradually led him to the love of man, who was first seen by him as a part of her mighty life, as a spirit embedded in the soul of the universe. He pierces through the bodily veil into the life within, which throbs to the pulsation of the Universal Heart. Thus man stands out grand, elemental, plain, against the spacious heavens of the poet's broad vision. He rises in superhuman magnitude above earthly dimensions, recedes into the mystic depths of limitless space, is glorified in the radiance of pure spirit.

> "The human nature unto which I felt
> That I belonged, and reverenced with love,
>   Was not a punctual presence, but a spirit
> Diffused through time and space." [1]

In a description which may be placed among Wordworth's most visionary and inspired pieces of poetry, he depicts to us the sight of the shepherd, as it suddenly flashes upon him amidst the gloom of the trackless hills.

> "A rambling schoolboy, thus
> I felt his presence (the shepherd's) in his own domain,
> As of a lord or master, or a power,
>   Or genius, under Nature, under God,
> Presiding, and severest solitude
> Had more commanding looks when he was there.

[1] *The Prelude* VIII, 608—610.

> When up the lonely brooks on rainy days
> Angling I went, or trod the trackless hills
> By mists bewildered, suddenly mine eyes
> Have glanced upon him distant a few steps,
> In size a giant, stalking through thick fog,
> His sheep like Greenland bears; or as he stepped
> Beyond the boundary line of some hill-shadow,
> His form hath flashed upon me, glorified
> By the deep radiance of the setting sun:
> Or him have I descried in distant sky,
> A solitary object and sublime,
> Above all height! like an aerial cross
> Stationed alone upon a spiry rock
> Of the Chartreuse, for worship." [1]

He is for ever grateful to Nature, through whose sanctifying medium he saw man thus, purified and hallowed, in his elemental grandeur, stripped of everything external. Thus his mind imbibed, at the time of his budding humanity, spiritual treasures, which are enduring even when the disillusioning aspects of man catch the eye and take possession of the soul. Therefore he did not despair, when in the great multitudes of London he caught sight of human deformity. The undercurrent of his soul's life was fed from the mystic Source which flowed at the dawn of his life, and which never ceased to shed its strength and its consolation into his receptive heart.

> "The Spirit of Nature was upon me there;
> The soul of Beauty and enduring Life
> Vouchsafed her inspiration, and diffused,
> Through meagre lines and colours, and the press
> Of self-destroying, transitory things,
> Composure, and ennobling Harmony." [2]

> "But though the picture weary out the eye,
> By nature an unmanageable sight,
> It is not wholly so to him who looks
> In steadiness, who hath among least things
> An under-sense of greatest; sees the parts
> As parts, but with a feeling of the whole." [3]

---

[1] *The Prelude* VIII, 256—275.
[2] *Ibid.* VII, 766—771.
[3] *Ibid.*, 731—737.

There came a time when humanity took precedence over nature in his affections. We have seen in the discussion of his nature-mysticism that through the intensity of the emotion with which nature inspired him, he was led to a belief in the power of the mind. She was to him the instrument through which the songs of the universe found expression. She was the medium through which the eternal world was revealed. In her God's strength and His solace are born along mystic ways to man's salvation.

> "There are in our existence spots of time,
> That with distinct pre-eminence retain
> A renovating virtue, whence, depressed
> By false opinion and contentious thought,
> Or aught of heavier or more deadly weight,
> In trivial occupations, and the round
> Of ordinary intercourse, our minds
> Are nourished and invisibly repaired;
> A virtue, by which pleasure is enhanced,
> That penetrates, enables us to mount,
> When high, more high, and lifts us up when fallen." [1]

The mind after all presides over nature in endowing her with the peculiar atmosphere in which she is steeped. From earliest childhood moments of the predominance of the mind over nature have been scattered through the poet's life. Some incidents which testify to the power of mind are related in *The Prelude*. One day he and an old servant of his father's ascended the hills on horseback. By some mischance they were separated, and the boy came upon a place, where in former times a murderer had been hanged. The gibbet-mast had fallen through decay, but on the turf hard by some unknown hand had carved the murderer's name. In a glimpse of awful realization the terror of the fact and of the place took hold of him, and he fled, horrified, ignorant of the road.

And the atmosphere of the boy's mind is transfused into the surrounding moorland, into the naked pool, the lonely figure of the pitcher-bearing girl forcing her way against the blowing storm, her clothes wind-tossed. All the dreariness and vague terror of

---

[1] *The Prelude* XII, 208—219.

his soul hangs in cloudy gloom over the face of nature, it has taken bodily form in her, and she is immaterialized by the impalpable atmosphere of soul, which dissolves corporeal distinctions into the limitless space of spiritual Being.

A proof of how important a part the mind plays in the creation of the atmosphere of the external world is the fact that this same moorland looked glad in the golden gleam of youth, when, with the loved one at his side, he walked across it in the exultation of early passion.

Another time he went forth into the fields to wait for the horses that were to take him and his brothers home for their Christmas-holidays. On the top of a crag, half-sheltered by a naked wall, on his right hand a single sheep, on his left a blasted hawthorn, in the midst of the wild tempestuousness of a gloomy day, he sat in passionate transports of expectation of the happy days to come. But instead of the expected joy, grief was to meet him in the paternal home. During those holidays, so fervently wished for, his father died, and he and his little brothers, now orphans, followed him to the grave. This event proved to be a source of deeply mystical experience to the boy Wordsworth. Through it was borne in upon him a sense of human dependence and of divine Power. It was his Gethsemane, where he learned to lay the whole of his life in the hands of Him Who encloses all in the power of His mind; and the place where the boy's heart had fluttered in joyous expectation, became invested with the mystic depth of his soul's experience, and often he repaired thither to drink as at a fountain the wisdom of transcendental teachings.

> "And, afterwards, the wind and sleety rain,
> And all the business of the elements,
> The single sheep, and the one blasted tree,
> And the bleak music from that old stone wall,
> The noise of wood and water, and the mist
> That on the line of each of those two roads
> Advanced in such indisputable shapes;
> All these were kindred spectacles and sounds
> To which I oft repaired, and thence would drink
> As at a fountain." [1]

[1] *The Prelude* XII, 317—326.

A very imposing example of Wordsworth's deeply mystical vision of man is contained in the description of the meeting with the solitary soldier in the peaceful quiet of the night after a time of frivolous enjoyment.

> "He was of stature tall,
> A span above man's common measure, tall,
> Stiff, lank and upright."
> . . . .
> "Companionless,
> No dog attending, by no staff sustained,
> He stood, and in his very dress appeared
> A desolation, a simplicity,
> To which the trappings of a gaudy world
> Make a strange back-ground. From his lips, ere long,
> Issued low muttered sounds, as if of pain
> Or some uneasy thought; yet still his form
> Kept the same awful steadiness — at his feet
> His shadow lay, and moved not." [1]

At last the poet, fascinated by the mysterious aloofness of the enigmatical figure, leaves his hiding-place beneath the hawthorn-bush and asks the stranger's history, and then in an unmoved manner

> "And with a quiet uncomplaining voice,
> A stately air of mild indifference,
> He told in few plain words a soldier's tale —
> That in the Tropic Islands he had served,
> Whence he had landed scarcely three weeks past;
> That on his landing he had been dismissed,
> And now was travelling towards his native home." [2]

The poet, moved with pity, asks the soldier to come with him, and so he continues his way, the stranger's "ghostly figure moving at his side," and in all the latter said

> "There was a strange half-absence, as of one
> Knowing too well the importance of his theme,
> But feeling it no longer." [3]

---

[1] *The Prelude* IV, 391—408.
[2] *Ibid.*, 419—426.
[3] *Ibid.*, 443—445.

On reaching a cottage, the poet commends him to the care of its inhabitants, telling them the story of the lonely, friendless man, at the same time enjoining upon the latter not to linger in the public ways henceforth, but ask for timely help.

> "At this reproof
> With the same ghastly mildness in his look,
> He said, 'My trust is in the God of Heaven,
> And in the eye of him who passes me!' " [1]

These last words are the quintessence of the mysterious wonder which precedes. The enigmatical stranger is as the embodiment of the enigma of solitude, which is the emptiness of the world and the fullness of God, the solitude which the mystic bears as heavenly grace in the inmost recess of his heart.

One of the poems in which this mystic vision of man is most perfectly conceived and expressed is *The Leechgatherer* or *Resolution and Independence*.

The lonely man on the lonely moor "beside a pool bare to the eye of Heaven," stands out in majesty of human strength and pious trustfulness. He towers up, giant-like, in sublime aloofness from the world's worry, in mystic blending with the soul of Nature, against the infinite space of God's silent heavens. The poet, who in weakness of faith had fallen from the height of his soul's rapture, which was an echo to nature's exultation on that wondrously beautiful spring-morning, when he set out towards the hills, saw in him a messenger sent from Heaven to teach him through his sublime serenity of soul, through his profound faith in life, God's wisdom, which is in the silence of the heart. The description of the man is highly imaginative. By comparing him to a huge stone on a hill-top, to a motionless cloud, Wordsworth gives expression to the cosmic vision which he had of the man. Nature and man are blended in mystical correlation. The lifeless stone is inspired with life, the man is endowed with the elemental grandeur of natural phenomena, losing the extraneous elements of humanity.

> "Now, whether it were by peculiar grace,
> A leading from above, a something given,

[1] *The Prelude IV*, 457—461.

> Yet it befell that, in this lonely place,
> When I with these untoward thoughts had striven,
> Beside a pool bare to the eye of heaven
> I saw a Man before me unawares:
> The oldest man he seemed that ever wore grey hairs.
>
> As a huge stone is sometimes seen to lie
> Couched on the bald top of an eminence;
> Wonder to all who do the same espy,
> By what means it could thither come, and whence;
> So that it seems a thing endued with sense:
> Like a sea-beast crawled forth, that on a shelf
> Of rock or sand reposeth, there to sun itself;
>
> Such seemed this Man, not all alive nor dead,
> Nor all asleep — in his extreme old age:
> His body was bent double, feet and head
> Coming together in life's pilgrimage;
> As if some dire constraint of pain, or rage
> Of sickness felt by him in times long past,
> A more than human weight upon his frame had cast.
>
> Himself he propped, limbs, body and pale face,
> Upon a long grey staff of shaven wood:
> And, still as I drew near with gentle pace,
> Upon the margin of that moorish flood
> Motionless as a cloud the old Man stood,
> That heareth not the loud winds when they call;
> And moveth all together, if it move at all."

And this man was stirring the pond with his staff. On the poet's inquiry the old man in stately speech

> "Such as grave Livers do in Scotland use,
> Religious men, who give to God and man their dues,"

told him, how he roamed from pond to pond in order to gather leeches, housing with God's help, where an opportunity offered, in this way gaining an honest livelihood.

Now the miracle begins to work upon the poet:

> "The old Man still stood talking by my side;
> But now his voice to me was like a stream
> Scarce heard; nor word from word could I divide;
> And the whole body of the Man did seem

> Like one whom I had met with in a dream;
> Or like a man from some far region sent,
> To give me human strength, by apt admonishment."

The poet's uneasy thoughts about the uncertain future of artists return again. He thought of Chatterton, "the marvellous Boy,

> The sleepless Soul that perished in his pride;
> Of Him who walked in glory and in joy
> Following his plough, along the mountain side,"

poets who began life in the strength and glory of their budding genius, and who ended it in the gloom of failure and despondency. From the anxiety of his heart the question rises again:

> "How is it that you live, and what is it you do?"

at which the old man repeats that he lives from the produce of the leeches, for the gathering of which he searches the ponds in the country, adding in startling calmness and firmness of mind:

> "Once I could meet with them on every side;
> But they have dwindled long by slow decay;
> Yet still I persevere, and find them where I may."

And the poet is stirred again by vague emotions, shadowy intuitions, and the man is seen in his mind's eye as a lonely spirit blending with the solitude of the weary moors.

> "While he was talking thus the lonely place,
> The old Man's shape, and speech — all troubled me:
> In my mind's eye I seemed to see him pace
> About the weary moors continually,
> Wandering about alone and silently."

And when the man has ended his story, spoken with such a dignity and superhuman cheerfulness of mind, the poet has entered the realms of true vision and exclaims in clarity of insight:

> "I could have laughed myself to scorn to find
> In that decrepit Man so firm a mind.
> 'God,' said I, 'be my help and stay secure;
> I'll think of the Leech-gatherer on the lonely moor.'"

In *The White Doe of Rylstone* the mystic feeling is not only felt as a soul's experience, but as a force which transforms values of lower order into treasures of the highest worth. "Everything," says Wordsworth, "that is attempted by the principal personages in *The White Doe* fails, so far as its object is external and substantial. So far as it is moral and spiritual it succeeds."

The struggle of Emily is like the laborious ascent towards the mountain-top, where the noises of the world die down and God's voice is heard in the silence of the unfathomable sky. There is a Christlike sanctity about her who knows how to transform worldly failure into spiritual triumph. In her have been fulfilled God's promises that he who endures to the end to him shall be given the crown of life, and that he who loses his life shall save it. She had been robbed of all that made life dear to her, but she was strong and worthy of the grace of God, thus filling her destined place:

> "A Soul, by force of sorrows high,
> Uplifted to the purest sky
> Of undisturbed humanity!" [1]

> "held above
> The infirmities of mortal love;
> Undaunted, lofty, calm, and stable,
> And awfully impenetrable." [2]

"A note of almost oriental renunciation runs through the poem. Human endeavour, the whole fabric of human deeds, are destined to pass away and leave no trace. Only Nature and Mind and the Peace of God endure. Salvation is not found through acting, but through suffering." [3]

In the lines prefixed to the poem, Wordsworth expresses in epitome the essence of the spiritual truth which is revealed in it:

> "Action is transitory — a step, a blow,
> The motion of a muscle — this way or that —
> 'Tis done; and in the after-vacancy
> We wonder at ourselves like men betrayed:
> Suffering is permanent, obscure and dark,

---

[1] *The White Doe of Rylstone* II, 585—588.
[2] *Ibid.* VII. 1625—1629.
[3] Harper, *William Wordsworth, etc.* II, p. 155.

And has the nature of infinity.
Yet through that darkness (infinite though it seem
And irremoveable) gracious openings lie,
By which the soul — with patient steps of thought
Now toiling, wafted now on wings of prayer —
May pass in hope, and though from mortal bonds
Yet undelivered, rise with sure ascent
Even to the fountain-head of peace divine." [1]

It is characteristic of Wordsworth, the worshipper of nature, that he should symbolize the soul's transcendental companionship in the figure of the white doe, one of nature's pure and lovely children. In the image of the animal as it passes in a gleam of whiteness through the poem is embodied the ultimate serenity and unworldliness of mind in which the mystic lives.

Those who think that Wordsworth had no eye for the tragic issues of life should read this poem. "If he believed that his earthly office was that of a comforter, it was because he felt how greatly men stood in need of consolation." [2] Not because he did not see sorrow, but because he felt it so very keenly, was his poetry in its ultimate value so joy-giving, just as the greatest drama ever enacted in the world became its most luminous gospel.

"If he consoles us it is because at times he has been disconsolate." [3]

"There is no lack here of the sense of Fate. That the poet should thus address himself calmly to scale these dizzy cliffs of anguish where the mortal senses reel, might almost seem too presumptuous an attempt for the powers of the human imagination. Wordsworth would never have dared it had not his own feelings on the death of his brother John given him guidance in the ascent." [4]

---

[1] The first six lines are quoted from the Tragedy of *The Borderers*, Act III, scene V, 1539—1544. The entire passage was added in 1837.
[2] Legouis, *La Jeunesse de William Wordsworth*, p. 389.
[3] Harper, *William Wordsworth*, etc. p. 157.
[4] Raleigh, *Wordsworth*, p. 193.

CHAPTER XIV

CONCLUSION

On comparing the two poets [1] we shall see that there is great affinity in their conception of *The Child*. Both thought the child to be endowed with a superior insight, both thought it to enjoy a supreme happiness owing to its mystic sensitiveness. But I am inclined to say that Blake's children on the whole are more childlike. Blake loses his own personality in the child's. He is a child with the children, is completely merged in their being, and he creates poetry which embodies the pure essence of the child's soul directly, without intermediary from the side of the poet. Wordsworth remains himself and is felt throughout as a presence that shapes, reflects and philosophizes. [2]

Francis Thompson, in his beautiful prose-poem on Shelley, ascribes the great fascination of his poetry to the childlike attitude of the poet's mind. He gives us his vision of the child with uncommon tenderness and deep intuitive grasp of the infinity of the child's imaginative power, impulsive vitality and rejoicing capacity.

"Know you what it is to be a child? It is to be something very different from the man of to-day. It is to have a spirit yet streaming from the waters of baptism, it is to believe in love, to believe in loveliness, to believe in belief, it is to be so little that the elves can reach to whisper in your ear, it is to turn pumpkins into coaches and mice into horses, lowness into loftiness and nothing into everything, for each child has its fairy-godmother in its own soul; it is to live in a nutshell and to count yourself king of infinite space, it is

[1] Crabb Robinson and Berger already drew attention to a certain affinity between Blake and Wordsworth.
[2] See Berger, *William Blake, etc.*, pp. 334—338.

CONCLUSION 155

> 'To see a world in a grain of sand,
> A Heaven in a wild flower,
> Hold infinity in the palm of your hand,
> And eternity in an hour,'
>
> it is to know not as yet that you are under a sentence of life, nor petition that it be commuted unto death. When we become conscious in dreaming that we dream, the dream is on the point of breaking, when we become conscious in living that we live, the ill dream is but just beginning."

And I am inclined to think that the spirit of this poetry lives stronger in Blake's child than in Wordsworth's. We have seen that with Wordsworth the great propelling force of the child is nature. Blake's child is also a nurseling of nature, but it enjoys her life more unconsciously. It delights in her happy sights and sounds, its life dances to the rhythm of her music, but a sense of mystery, of undefinable awe, of dim adumbrations of "a Creature moving about in worlds not realized" which nature inspires in the child Wordsworth does not rise to its consciousness. So we might say that Wordsworth's child has a profounder intuitive knowledge of nature's mystic depth. To Wordworth's child nature is all in all, to Blake's child it is not. It possesses the added treasure of faith in Christ, which illumines its life with an enhanced glory, and which is born of its experience of sorrow, which, like its consolation, is of an exquisite tenderness and gleaming emotional sweetness. We might almost say that Blake's child is more pious than Wordsworth's but then, when I consider the exalted happiness, the crystalline purity, the emotional profundity of the experience of the child Wordsworth, I cannot but believe that its grasp of Universal Life was so deep as to make it, just like Blake's child, partaker of the mystery of divine Love. Besides, the belief in the incarnation, which Blake expresses in such poems as *The Lamb* and the *Cradle-Song*, is not so much the belief in the historical birth, and earthly life of Christ, as a faith in an ever-renewed pouring out of God's Spirit in the world, consequently a belief in divine immanence, and was not this the creed of the child Wordsworth? "The one secret, the greatest of all," says Patmore, another English poet-mystic, "is the doctrine of the Incarnation, regarded not as an historical event which occurred two thousand years ago, but as an event which is renewed in the body of every one who is in the way to the fulfilment of his original destiny." [1]

We also see affinity between Blake and Wordsworth with respect to their conception of *Nature and the Imagination*. We noticed that to Blake the imagination is all, that only in her is life, vision, that only the eye of the imagination can look through nature into supernature, reality. We saw that Wordsworth, too, believed in the superior power of the imagination as the faculty which leads us to the heights of spiritual life. But the great difference between the two mystics is this, that Wordsworth was led through nature to his belief in the imagination, that there was a reciprocal action going on between the two; nature was even in his old age, when she denied him mystic union with her, an object of sacred reverence, because without her he might never have attained to the high uplands of god-possessed existence. Wordsworth's belief in the imagination was born of nature's emotional power, Blake's belief in it existed independent of nature. But in moments when her beauty, her life, appealed to him, she, too, was taken up into the transfusing glow of imaginative creation. Blake is an angel, fallen into the world of division, and sorrowing under a sense of loss, Wordsworth is a loving child of his mother earth, whose "vast heart" he felt beating with "warm, wild mother-love," in the glow of which he mounted to the land of his desires. Filled with a sense of grace bestowed on him, he paced the transitory world as a blessed spirit in the sheen of the eternal day. With Wordsworth the imagination ascends through nature to her supernatural home; with Blake she descends from the supernal regions into the visible world. Symons says: "Where other poets use reality as a springboard into space, Blake uses it as a foothold on his return from flight," [2] and of these other poets Wordsworth may be considered a good representative.

In a copy of Wordsworth's works, Blake wrote: "Natural objects always did and now do weaken and deaden and obliterate imagination in me. Wordsworth must know that what he writes valuable is not to be found in nature. I see in Wordworth the natural man

---

[1] Coventry Patmore, *The Rod, the Root and the Flower*, quoted by Evelyn Underhill in *Mysticism*, p. 141.
See A. Charles Babenroth, *English Childhood*, Ch. VI, VII.
[2] Symons, *William Blake*, p. 78.

rising up against the spiritual, and then he is no poet, but a Heathen Philosopher.

> 'And I could wish my days to be
> Bound each to each by natural piety.'

There is no such thing as natural piety, because the natural man is at enmity with God."

Wordsworth's ultimate vision was one of the supremacy of the imagination, transcending nature, yet immanent in it, and was not this Blake's belief? But the latter was often caught in the one-sidedness of his mind. He, the vehement visionary, could be so uniquely possessed by one idea that anything which seemed to be in contradiction to it was thrown out as inconsistent, and thus be often belied his own assertions. On the other hand he praised Wordsworth as a great man, as the only poet of the age. Under the verses *To H. C., six years old* he wrote: "This is all in the highest degree imaginative and equal to any poet, but not superior. I cannot think that real poets have any competition. None are greatest in the Kingdom of Heaven. It is so in poetry." We know, too, that Wordsworth appreciated him. In a letter to Dorothy Wordsworth Crabb Robinson said: "I gave your brother some poems in M. S. by him, and they interested him — as well they might, for there is an affinity between them, as there is between the regulated imagination of a wise poet and the incoherent dreams of a poet." [1] I cannot but regret Blake's somewhat forced deification of the imagination at the expense of nature; it tended towards deadening his natural creative energy, to which we owe poetry of the highest quality.

We have seen that Wordsworth expressed a *Belief in a prenatal Existence of the Soul*, most definitely in the *Ode on Immortality*. Blake admired this poem very much, the parts which he most enjoyed being the most obscure and those which Crabb Robinson liked and comprehended the least.

Though Blake's vision of childhood did not lead him to a belief in a prior existence, yet we know that he believed in an ante-natal reality of purely spiritual life. The central doctrine of the *Prophetic*

---

[1] Crabb Robinson, *Letter to Dorothy Wordsworth*, 20 Febr. 1826.

Books turns on this. The fall of Urizen is the fall of spiritual man into the world of matter.

Crabb Robinson writes in his *Reminiscences:* "As I had for many years been familiar with the idea that an eternity 'a parte post' was inconceivable with an eternity "a parte ante," he brightened and he eagerly assented: 'To be sure we are all coexistent with God, members of the Divine Body, and partakers of the Divine Nature.'"

The belief of Blake and Wordsworth in a pre-natal existence leads me to the discussion of their *Belief in Immortality*.

In Blake's poetry there is always an underground of melancholy. Perfect bliss is after all only to be obtained, when we shall have done away with our mortal bodies and shall be taken up in the world of pure spirit. Death had nothing dark, nothing mysterious for him. We might almost say that the thought of its coming deliverance was his greatest consolation. I spoke about his marvellous, ecstatic dying, which was entirely inspired by the consciousness of nearing his true life. He sang of his vision so rapturously:

> "The Door of Death is made of gold
> That Mortal eyes cannot behold;
> But when the mortal eyes are clos'd
> And cold and pale the Limbs repos'd,
> The soul awakes; and, wond'ring, sees
> In her mild hand the golden Keys:
> The Grave is Heaven's Golden Gate,
> And rich and poor around it wait;
> O Shepherdess of England's fold,
> Behold this Gate of Pearl and Gold!"[1]

Wordworth's belief in immortality was not so shining, not so predominant as Blake's. It was as a deep consolation hidden in his vision of God, a consolation in the mystery of the brooding doom. As everything in Wordsworth with respect to Blake this belief, too, is more permeated with the breath of humanity. These words of consolation the wanderer speaks to the despondent solitary:

> "I cannot doubt that they whom you deplore
> Are glorified; or, if they sleep shall wake
> From sleep, and dwell with God in endless love.

[1] *To the Queen*, Dedication to the Illustrations of Blair's *Grave*.

> Hope, below this, consists not with belief
> In mercy, carried infinite degrees
> Beyond the tenderness of human hearts:
> Hope, below this, consists not with belief
> In perfect wisdom, guiding mightiest power,
> That finds no limits but her own pure will." [1]

The belief in immortality is expressed more beautifully, in a less sermonizing way, in the after-thought of the *Duddon-Sonnets*, where we hear the grave wisdom of the poet, who feeds on the immortal power of the imagination, which instills in him the exalted faith of unknown possibilities beyond the silent grave:

> "Enough, if something from our hands have power
> To live, and act, and serve the future hour;
> And if, as toward the silent tomb we go,
> Through love, through hope, and faith's transcendent dower,
> We feel that we are greater than we know."

On the grave of his little boy Thomas, who died in 1812, the mourning father wrote the prayer:

> Six months to six years added he remained
> Upon this sinful earth, by sin unstained:
> O blessèd Lord, whose mercy then removed
> A Child whom every eye that looked on loved;
> Support us, teach us, calmly to resign
> What we possessed, and now is wholly thine!"

We feel the great difference in tone, in mentality between Blake and Wordsworth.

The above-mentioned quotations from Wordsworth bear the stamp of the attitude towards the Christian faith in his later years. Earlier in 1799, in one of the exquisite *Lucy-poems*, he sang the mystic lines of the pantheist:

> "A slumber did my spirit seal;
> I had no human fears:
> She seemed a thing that could not feel
> The touch of earthly years.

---

[1] *The Excursion* IV, 188—197.

> No motion has she now, no force;
>   She neither hears nor sees;
> Rolled round in earth's diurnal course,
>   With rocks, and stones, and trees."

In a different spirit again the belief is expressed in *We are Seven*, where it is born of the child's intuitive power; we saw that the same spirit inspires the great *Ode*. In the beauty of nature the boy-Wanderer felt everything to breathe immortality.

We have seen in the course of my essay that both Blake and Wordsworth, as true mystics, exalted *The Imagination*, the intuitive power, above reason.

It is the principal subject of Blake's song, the glorification of the divine imagination and the denunciation of the dead intellect.

In *A Poet's Epitaph* Wordsworth gives in epitome his opinion on the value of analytical, uninspired intellectualism. He ridicules in subtle satire the philosopher and the moralist, who, caught in their own littleness, cannot lift themselves beyond the world of dead fact and try to solve all questions by means of uninspired intellect. They are not allowed to desecrate with their uncongenial analysis the poet's grave:

> "Physician, art thou? – one, all eyes,
> Philosopher! – a fingering slave,
> One that would peep and botanize
> Upon his mother's grave?
>
> Wrapt closely in thy sensual fleece,
> O turn aside, – and take, I pray,
> That he below may rest in peace,
> Thy ever-dwindling soul, away!
>
> A Moralist perchance appears;
> Led, Heaven knows how! to this poor sod:
> And he has neither eyes nor ears;
> Himself his world, and his own God;
>
> One to whose smooth-rubbed soul can cling
> Nor form, nor feeling, great or small;
> A reasoning, self-sufficing thing,
> An intellectual All-in-all!
>
> Shut close the door; press down the latch;
> Sleep in thy intellectual crust;

> Nor lose ten tickings of thy watch
> Near this unprofitable dust."

We recognize in it Blake's attitude towards Urizen, Locke and Newton.

I have now compared Blake's and Wordsworth's mysticism on certain subjects. When we put them opposite each other in general outline, we moreover see that in Wordsworth, when he is mystically inspired, we always feel the man, the man who is deeply moved, violently stirred at the revelation which is consummated, dazzlingly luminious in the unsearchable depths of his soul. There is always a sense of awe, of mystery, even in the moments of clearest insight and most exalted serenity. Blake is almost spirit with the spirits, he nearly loses his human identity in the presence of his visions which his mystical senses see emerging from the world of reality. Blake is often so familiar with the spiritual world, that the communion with her does not move him exceptionally. Blake had often moods in which he could say:

> "Thou art a man, God is no more:
> Thy own humanity learn to adore," [1]

words which do not convey any emotion at the experience of God's immanence in the creature. In the *Prophetic Books* Blake is the prophet, who sees in visible shape the ultimate union of the soul with God, but he does not reveal the union, he does not speak of the inner experience as Wordsworth, who always emerges from his immersion in visionary light with something of the holiness of God, of His purity and His wisdom. Vision makes Wordsworth a better man. His vision is chiefly emotional, Blake's more intellectual. Wordsworth is nearer to the "secret place which the mystic knows, where God without form of words or speech declares all Truth." [2] He is more akin to the great classical mystics. Vision meant to him increase of moral strength. Its light, once shed in complete illumination, continues to shine on the path of man and to show

---

[1] *The Everlasting Gospel*.
[2] Maynard, *The mystical Note in Poetry*. (The Poetry Review VII, 1916.) Maynard does not consider Blake a mystic.

him the way to a life in accordance with the deepest feelings, the holiest thoughts, which the moment of initiation into the supernal world enclosed. This is the great difference between Wordsworth and Blake. Hutton has said that Wordsworth alone of all the great men of his day had seen "the light of the countenance of God shining clear into the face of duty," not duty as a mechanical obedience to outward law, but as the spontaneous acting up to the dictates of the highest will. Wordsworth's vision drew the whole life of man into its sphere. He saw its light shining forth from the face of the earth and he saw it brighten in the countenances of his fellow-men, whom he saw symbolised in their most elemental form in the humble dalesmen of the land of his birth, the bearers of "the impersonated thought, the idea or abstraction of the kind." He saw its light not as a momentary flash, but as an illumination of their simple lives, a sanctification of their daily work. It was a comfort to Margaret in her distress, it gave the Wanderer his exalted serenity of mind, it revealed to Michael that

> "There is a comfort in the strength of love;
> 'T will make a thing endurable, which else
> Would overset the brain, or break the heart." [1]

Blake does not see life in this manner. He focusses everything on the inspired moment, which means the vision of God, and which is not dependent on purity of heart, only on "the absolute affirmation of that energy which is eternal delight. Like Nietzsche, but with a deeper innocence, he finds himself 'beyond good and evil.'" [2] "Men are admitted to Heaven, because they have cultivated their understanding. The fool shall not enter into heaven, let him be ever so holy," he said in the *Vision of the last Judgment* and in *The Marriage of Heaven and Hell*: "I tell you, no virtue can exist without breaking the ten commandments. Jesus was all virtue and acted from impulse, not from rules." But Blake forgot that a holy man is never a fool, and that Jesus was in a sense beyond the temptation of ordinary man, that His life therefore could flow "according to its own sweet will" in the perfection of His Father's image.

[1] *Michael*, 448—451.
[2] Symons, *William Blake*, p. 80.

A mystic greater than Blake has said: "What I would that do I not, but what I hate that do I." [1]

And another: "I was swept up to Thee by Thy Beauty, and torn away from Thee by my own weight." [2] We do not hear such a thing from Blake, the poet of the lines:

> "Abstinence sows sand all over
> The ruddy limbs and flaming hair,
> But Desire gratified
> Plants fruits of life and beauty there." [3]

In this he also differs from his spiritual masters, Swedenborg and Boehme, both of whom were conscious of their sinful tendencies. In his diary Swedenborg lays bare his inward struggle to attain to the spiritual level of a true Christian, from Boehme's lips we hear the fervent prayer of humble prostration before a holy God.

"In Blake we find no rejections, no disgusting temptations, terrible starvings or lashings of mind or flesh, no cult of filth; nothing morbid or ascetic whatsoever, not even a disposition towards solemnity or pitiful self-accusation. The normal life, heightened, was his ideal." [4]

In essence it is the ideal of all mystics, but most of them have felt that the road to a heightened existence lies through the renunciation of a lower one. Blake's unbounded energy of life, absolute absence of restriction, can only exist in his world of pure spirit. Because Wordsworth clings more to fact, is less abstract in his conceptions than Blake, his ethical force is much greater. And we do not conceive this in a sense of uninspired moralizing; Wordsworth's poetry abounds but too much in it to convince us that nothing but what is really alive, has ethical value.

We have seen that Blake dissolved the antithethis of *Art and Religion*, Wordsworth showed a tendency towards seeing one spirit in the two, at least in poetry and religion. With Blake the identity of art and religion was one of his fundamental beliefs, and he proclaimed it definitely and enthusiastically. With Words-

---

[1] *Romans* VII, 20.
[2] St. Augustine, *Confessions*, book VII, chapter XVII.
[3] *Gnomic Verses* from the Rossetti-manuscript.
[4] Foster Damon, *William Blake, etc.*, p. 10.

worth it was less essential, he did not express himself so decidedly about it, yet we have statements of his which prove the two poets to have had kindred opinions on the subject. In the essay supplementary to the preface to the second edition of the *Lyrical Ballads* he said that poetry was most just to its divine origin, when it administers and breathes the spirit of religion. To Lady Beaumont he wrote what was the office of his poems: "to console the afflicted, to add sunshine to daylight by making the happy happier, to teach the young and the gracious of every age to see, to think and feel, and therefore become more actively and securely virtuous." And is not this the task of the religious teacher in the highest and broadest sense of the word? He once said that anybody entirely devoid of a feeling for poetry could not be truly religious. "Poetry is the first and last of all knowledge — it is as immortal as the heart of man.... Poetry is the breath and finer spirit of all knowledge.... Poetry is the spontaneous overflow of powerful feeling.... What is a Poet? A man endowed with more lively sensibility, more enthusiasm and tenderness, who has a greater knowledge of human nature and a more comprehensive soul than are supposed to be common among mankind, a man who rejoices more than other men in the spirit of life that is in him." [2] In the last words we touch upon Blake's conception of unrestrained energy. With Wordsworth feeling is the first thing, it includes imagination; with Blake the imagination is all in all.

That Wordsworth fulfilled his ideal of being a religious teacher is testified by many lovers of his poetry. Because the spirit his poetry breathes is the spirit of religion, "his exponents," says Myers, "are not content to treat his poems on nature simply as graceful descriptive pieces, but they speak of him in terms usually reserved for the originators of some great religious movement." [3] "The very image of Wordsworth," says de Quincey, "as I prefigured it to my own planet-struck eye, crushed my faculties as before Elijah or St. Paul." [4] Stuart Mill experienced Wordsworth's consolatory, stimulating force, when he passed through the spir-

---

[1] *Letter to Lady Beaumont*, May 21st, 1807.
[2] *Preface to the second Edition of the Lyrical Ballads.*
[3] Myers, *Wordsworth*, p. 124.
[4] Quoted by Myers in *Wordsworth*, p. 124.

itual crisis of his life, when hope and belief in happiness failed him. "From them, (Wordsworth's poems) I seemed to learn what would be the perennial sources of happiness, when all the greater evils of life shall have been removed. And I felt myself at once better and happier as I came under their unfluence." [1]

Christopher North valued the *Lyrical Ballads* next to the Bible. It is told of an old Scotch shepherd, that besides his Bible he read Wordsworth's poetry. These utterances say much; they could not have been said of Blake. His is the more fiery, stormy mind, not so evenly-balanced. The struggle of his lonely life was a fierce one. The feeling of neglect, misunderstanding of his genius, of which he was so proudly conscious, gnawed at the inmost fibres of his heart, and he dreamt himself away from the earth in which he felt a lonely exile. Often, in violent endeavour to do so, with the force of tempest-madness, he rushed into the seething world of his imagination, snapping off the chords which bind us to the shining home of our humanity. Then we cannot follow him, he outflies our human ken, and probably his own.

The greatest visionaries, such as Dante, the writer of the Apocalypse, have not lost sight of the world in which we live, [2] their images are built up of the materials drawn from our earthly life, transfused by their visionary glow; their poetry, however visionary, however heavenly, is aflame with the spirit of humanity, Blake, in his endeavour to call forth images only from the creative ground of his imagination, often loses himself in an expressionless, vapoury, would-be spirituality. Wordsworth always remains within the boundary of human perception. His poetry may be less passionate, it may lack the swinging sweep of Blake's magic music, which carries us along self-lost in its enigmatic harmony, yet the subdued fire of Wordsworth's poetry has a power more penetrating, more abiding than Blake's. The spirit of it is woven round the passions, the feelings which form the life-blood of our inner existence. They are purified by it into the luminous steps along which we mount to the land of dreams. With Wordsworth the dream hangs round the common things of "mother earth."

[1] John Stuart Mill, *Autobiography*, quoted by Myers in *Wordsworth*, p. 136.
[2] See Berger, *William Blake, etc.*, pp. 306, 307.

> "Long have I loved what I behold,
> The night that calms, the day that cheers;
> The common growth of mother earth
> Suffices me — her tears, her mirth
> Her humblest mirth and tears." [1]

Blake is a stranger in the world of appearances and as long as his yearning for his lost paradise and his vision of it remains within human bonds, it gives birth to poetry which in its fervently yearning aspiration is among the very rare pearls of lyrical mysticism. I think of poems like the fragile *Land of Dreams*, a song laden with the fragrance of the sweetest devotion, in which we hear the hankering anguish of the world-strange pilgrim in the rare music of the little dreamer's words:

> "Father! O father! what do we here
> In this land of unbelief and fear?
> The land of Dreams is better far,
> Above the light of the morning star."

We do not find a thing of such colour and tone in Wordsworth. His mind was too self-possessed for it. This self-possession was his strength, especially his strength as a mystic, but on the other hand, because of it, we miss in him the lyrical cry of unattained aspiration. With Wordsworth the sense of loss, of brokenness and division is transmuted into the consciousness of mystic union. He sings of

> "Melancholy fear, subdued by Faith;
> Of blessed consolations in distress." [2]

The encumbrance of mortality is not ignored by Wordsworth, but its troubles are chased away

> "With only such degree of sadness left
> As may support longings of pure desire,
> And strengthen love, rejoicing secretly
> In the sublime attractions of the grave." [3]

---

[1] *Peter Bell, Prologue,* 131—136.
[2] *The Excursion, Introduction,* 15—17.
[3] *Ibid.* IV, 235—239.

CONCLUSION

The Wanderer in *The Excursion* is the mouthpiece of the redeeming force of mystic vision. After he has told the poet the tragic story of Margaret he says:

> "My Friend! enough to sorrow you have given,
> The purposes of wisdom ask no more:
> Nor more would she have craved as due to One
> Who, in her worst distress, had ofttimes felt
> The unbounded might of prayer; and learned, with soul
> Fixed on the Cross, that consolation springs,
> From sources deeper far than deepest pain,
> For the meek Sufferer." [1]

And afterwards:

> "I well remember that those very plumes,
> Those weeds, and the high spear-grass on that wall,
> By mist and silent rain-drops silvered o'er,
> As once I passed, into my heart conveyed
> So still an image of tranquillity,
> So calm and still, and looked so beautiful
> Amid the uneasy thoughts which filled my mind,
> That what we feel of sorrow and despair
> From ruin and from change, and all the grief
> That passing shows of Being leave behind,
> Appeared an idle dream, that could maintain,
> Nowhere, dominion o'er the enlightened spirit
> Whose meditative sympathies repose
> Upon the breast of Faith. I turned away
> And walked along my road in happiness." [2]

Here we have in a nutshell the secret of Wordsworth's optimism. Here we have a blending of the Christian's mystic salvation in the prayerful taking up of the Cross and the Platonic mysticism which mounts by way of the physical forms, the illusory world, to the land of Reality. It is a blending of the early Wordsworth and the later, of the worshipper of nature and the pious Christian. This note of serene unworldliness, of absolute harmony, of

---

[1] *The Excursion* I, 931—938.
[2] *Ibid.*, 942—957. See Irving Babbitt (Rousseau and Romanticism, p. 256), who says of this beautiful piece of poetry that it is "tampering with evil."

peaceful tranquillity, is not struck by Blake. The latter is haunted by a vision which he sees glimmering in the remote past of prenatal bliss, in the coming resurrection of dead Albion, in the hopeful promise of the home beyond the grave. Hence his yearning cry and his prophetic ecstacy.

> "And did the Countenance Divine
> Shine forth upon our clouded hills?
> And was Jerusalem builded here
> Among these dark Satanic Mills?
>
> Bring me my bow of burning gold!
> Bring me my arrows of desire!
> Bring me my spear! O clouds, unfold!
> Bring me my chariot of fire!
>
> I will not cease from mental fight,
> Nor shall my sword sleep in my hand,
> Till we have built Jerusalem
> In England's green and pleasant land." [1]

In things like this Blake is very great. There is a fire, a flow of energy in it, a rhythmical swing, a restless reaching out after the ideal, which is quite unique. He is the glowing prophet with the golden promise of coming bliss; Wordsworth is the serene singer of harmony attained, and if St. Augustine's experience that our heart is restless within us, until it finds rest in God, is true, I am inclined to think that Wordsworth was nearer to the central Heart of peace than Blake. When Watson stands by Wordsworth's grave in Grasmere Churchyard, where he and those who were so dear to him, slumber in the shady beauty of its sycamores, sung to rest by the lulling murmur of his beloved Rotha, near the "old rude church with bare, bald tower," yet in the midst of his hills, his lakes, his streams, the very peculiar flavour of his poetry, the exalted, godly peace it breathes, its healing and sustaining power, is strongly felt by him. I shall conclude with a quotation from the poem which expresses these feelings, it being my final valuation of the essence of Wordsworth's poetry, which is its mysticism.

---

[1] *Milton*, Preface.

CONCLUSION

"Poet, who sleepest by this wandering wave!
When thou wast born, what birthgift hadst thou then?
To thee what wealth was that the Immortals gave,
The wealth thou gavest in thy turn to men?

Not Milton's keen, translunar music thine;
Not Shakespeare's cloudless, boundless human view;
Not Shelley's flush of rose on peaks divine;
Nor yet the wizard twilight Coleridge knew.

What hadst thou that could make so large amends
For all thou hadst not and thy peers possessed,
Motion and fire, swift means to radiant ends? —
Thou hadst, for weary feet, the gift of rest.

From Shelly's dazzling glow or thunderous haze,
From Byron's tempest-anger, tempest-mirth,
Men turned to thee and found — *not blast and blaze
Tumult of tottering heavens, but peace on earth.* [1]

Nor peace that grows by Lethe, scentless flower,
There in white languors to decline and cease;
But peace whose names are also rapture, power,
Clear sight, and love: for these are parts of peace.
. . . .
Rest! 't was the gift *he* gave; and peace! the shade
He spread for spirits fevered with the sun.
To him his bounties are come back — here laid
In rest, in peace, his labour nobly done." [2]

---

[1] The italics are mine.
[2] William Watson, *Wordsworth's Grave*.

BIBLIOGRAPHY

JACOB BOEHME, *The Aurora*. Translated by J. Sparrow. London, 1914.
JACOB BOEHME, *The Way to Christ*. London, 1911.
C. K. CHESTERTON, *St. Francis of Assisi*. London, 1923.
MEISTER ECKEHART, *Schriften und Predigten*, aus dem Mittelhochdeutschen übersetzt und herausgegeben von Büttner. Leipzig, 1903.
ST. FRANCIS OF ASSISI, *The little Flowers of St. Francis of Assisi*, translated by T. W. Arnold. London, 1903.
PAUL HANKAMER, *Jacob Boehme, Gestalt und Gestaltung*. Bonn, 1924.
W. R. INGE, *Christian Mysticism*. London, 1899.
W. R. INGE, *Studies of English Mystics*. London, 1906.
WILLIAM JAMES, *The Varieties of Religious Experience: A study in Human Nature*. London, 1903.
THOMAS À KEMPIS, *De Navolging van Christus*, vertaald door Dr. Is. van Dijk. Haarlem, 1909.
MAURICE MAETERLINCK, *Le Trésor des Humbles*. Paris, 1902.
The Oxford Book of English Mystical Verse. Oxford, 1921.
JAN VAN RUYSBROECK, *L'ornement des Noces Spirituelles* de Ruysbroeck l'Admirable, trad. par Maurice Maeterlinck. Bruxelles, 1900.
PAUL SABATIER, *Vie de St. François d'Assise*. Paris, 43 ed., 1918.
CAROLINE F. E. SPURGEON, *Mysticism in English Literature*. Cambridge, 1913.
TROBRIDGE, *Emanuel Swedenborg*. London, 1920.
EVELYN UNDERHILL, *Mysticism: A Study in the Nature and Development of Man's spiritual Consciousness*. London, 1911.
EVELYN UNDERHILL, *The mystic Way*. London, 1913.
EVELYN UNDERHILL, *The Mystics of the Church*. London.

IRVING BABBITT, *Rousseau and Romanticism*. Boston and New York, 1919.
A. CHARLES BABENROTH, *English Childhood*. New York, 1922.
Publications of the Blake-Society. Thomas Wright, Olney, 1912.
    SIR WILLIAM BLAKE, *Chairman's Address*.
    THOMAS WRIGHT, *Secretary's Address*.
    GREVILLE MACDONALD, *William Blake, the practical Idealist*.
    HERBERT JENKINS, *The Teaching of William Blake*.
    WALTER K. JEALOUS, *Hampstead in the time of Blake*.
    G. H. LEONARD, *The Art of William Blake*.
    F. C. OWLETT, *Blake's Burden*.

BIBLIOGRAPHY

ADELINE BUTTERWORTH, *William Blake, Mystic.*Liverpool and London, 1911.
OSBERT BURDETT, *William Blake.* London, 1926.
HAROLD BRUCE, *William Blake in this World.* London, 1925.
G. K. CHESTERTON, *William Blake,* London, 1910.
EDWIN J. ELLIS AND WILLIAM BUTLER YEATS, *The Works of William Blake, Poetic, Symbolic and Critical.* London, 1893.
EDWIN J. ELLIS, The real Blake. London, 1907.
ALEXANDER GILCHRIST, *The Life of William Blake.* London, 1863.
LAFCADIO HEARN, *Interpretations of Literature.* London, 1916.
JAMES G. HUNEKER, *Egoists:* A Book of Supermen. London, 1909.
RUDOLF KASSNER, *William Blake: die Mystik, die Künstler und das Leben, über Englische Dichter und Maler im 19 Jahrhundert,* Leipzig, 1900.
GEOFFREY KEYNES, Bibliography of William Blake, New-York, 1921.
GREVILLE MACDONALD, *The Sanity of William Blake.* London, 1908.
E. R. D. MACLAGAN and A. G. B. RUSSELL, *Jerusalem.* London, 1904. *Milton,* London, 1907.
P. H. OSMOND, *The Mystical Poets of the English Church.* London, 1919.
HENRY CRABB ROBINSON, *Blake Coleridge, Wordsworth, Lamb, etc., being selections from the Remains of H. C. R.,* edited by Edith J. Morley. Manchester, 1922.
JOHN SAMPSON, *The poetical Works of William Blake,* edited with an Introduction and Textual Notes. Oxford, 1914.
DENIS SAURAT, *Blake and Milton.* Bordeaux, 1907.
BASIL DE SELINCOURT, *William Blake.* London, 1909.
D. J. SLOSS and J. P. R. WALLIS, *The Prophetic Writings of William Blake,* edited with a general Introduction, glossarial Index of Symbols, Commentary and Appendices. Oxford, 1926.
ALFRED STORY, *William Blake: His Life, Character and Genius.* London, 1893.
ALGERNON CHARLES SWINBURNE, *William Blake : A critical Essay.* London, 1868.
ARTHUR SYMONS, *William Blake.* London 1907.
> It contains contemporary biographies:
> BENJAMIN HEATH MALKIN, *A Father's Memoirs of his Child,* 1806.
> LADY CHARLOTTE BURY, *Diary,* 1820.
> *Blake's Horoscope,* Urania, 1825.
> VARLEY, *A Treatise on Zodiacal Physiognomy,* 1828.
> JOHN THOMAS SMITH, *Biographical Sketch of Blake* from *The Memoirs.* 1828.
> ALLAN CUNNINGHAM, *The Life of William Blake* from *Lives of the most eminent British Painters, Sculptors, and Architects,* 1830.
> Henry Crabb Robinson, Extracts from *The Diary, Letters and Reminiscences of H. C. R.* 1810—1852.
FREDERICK TATHAM, *The Life of William Blake,* printed with *Letters of William Blake,* edited by Archibald G. B. Russell. London, 1906.
OTTO VON TAUBE, *William Blake, die Ethik der Fruchtbarkeit.* Jena, 1907.

GARTH WILKINSON, *Introduction to the Songs of Innocence and Experience.* London, 1839.
HELEN C. WHITE, *The Mysticism of William Blake.* Madison, 1927.
WILLIAM BUTLER YEATS, *Ideas of Good and Evil.* London, 1917.

FRANÇOIS BÉNOIT, *William Blake, the Mystic*, Annals of Psychichal Science. Jan. 1908.
A. K. C, *An Analysis of Blake's Attitude to War*, The poetry Review VI, 1916.
A. CLUTTON—BROCK, *Blake as a Prophet*, The London Mercury I, 3.
JEANNE DOIN, *William Blake*, Gazette des beaux Arts, ser. 4, VII, 1912.
K. A. ESDAILE, *An early Appreciation of William Blake*, The Library, ser. 3, V, 1914.
WILLIAM NORMAN GUTHRIE, *William Blake, Mystic*, Sewanee Review V, 1897.
HENRY G. HEWLETT, *Imperfect Genius: William Blake*, Contemporary Review XXVIII, Oct. 1876, XXIX, Jan. 1877.
CHARLES HIGHAM, *Blake and the Swedenborgians*, Notes and Queries XI, Jan., June 1915.
GREVILLE MACDONALD, *William Blake, his Critics and Masters*, The Vineyard, June 1911.
THEODORE MAYNARD, *The mystic Note in Poetry*, The Poetry Review VII, 1916.
H. N. MORRIS, *Blake and Swedenborg*, The Quest, Oct. 1919.
FREDERICK E. PIERCE, *Blake and seventeenth century Authors*, Modern Language Notes XXXIX, 1924.
THE REV. RICHARD ROBERTS, *The Ethics of William Blake*, The Hibbert Journal XVII, 1919.
HENRY CRABB ROBINSON, *William Blake, Artist, Poet and Religious Mystic*, Vaterländisches Museum, 1811.
THEODORE T. STENBERG, *Blake's Indebtedness to the "Eddas,"* The Modern Language Review II, Apr. 1923.
STEPHAN ZWEIG, *William Blakes Auferstehung*, Beilage der Neue freie Presse, 1907.

MATTHEW ARNOLD, *Essays in Criticism.* London, 1888.
MATTHEW ARNOLD, *Memorial Verses*, 1850.
WALTER BAGEHOT, *Literary Studies. Article on Wordsworth, Tennyson and Browning.* London, 1864. Every Man's Library.
MARJORIE BARSTOW, *Wordsworth's Theory of poetic Diction, A Study of the historical and personal Background of the Lyrical Ballads.* New Haven, 1917.
ARTHUR BEATTY, *William Wordsworth, his Doctrine and Art in their historical Relations.* -Madison, 1922.
K. W. BÖMIG, *Wordsworth im Urteile seiner Zeit.* Leipzig, 1906.

BIBLIOGRAPHY

A. C. BRADLEY, *Oxford Lectures on Poetry*. London, 1909.
G. BRANDES, *Die Hauptströmungen der Literatur des neunzehnten Jahrhunderts* IV. Berlin, 1900—1914.
ALOIS BRANDL, *Samuel Taylor Coleridge und die Englische Romantik*. Strassburg, 1886.
STOPFORD A. BROOKE, *Naturalism in English Poetry*. London, 1902.
OLIVER ELTON, *Wordsworth*, London, 1924.
H. W. GARROD, *Wordsworth: Lectures and Essays*. Oxford, 1923.
MARIE GOTHEIN, *William Wordsworth, sein Leben, seine Werke, seine Zeitgenossen*. Halle, 1893.
GEORGE MCLEAN HARPER, *William Wordsworth, his Life, his Work and Influence*. London, 1916.
GEORGE MCLEAN HARPER, *Wordsworth's French Daughter*. London and Princeton, 1921.
WILLIAM HAZLITT, *The Spirit of the Age*. 1825.
C. H. HERFORD, *The Age of Wordsworth*. London, 1897.
B. H. HUTTON, *Literary Essays*. London, 1871.
WILLIAM KNIGHT, *The Life of William Wordsworth*. Edinburgh, 1889.
Wordsworthiana, Papers read to the Wordsworth-society, edited by William Knight. London, 1889.
Letters of the Wordsworth Family, collected and edited by William Knight. Boston and London, 1907.
ÉMILE LEGOUIS, *The early Life of William Wordsworth*, translated by J. W. Matthews. London, 1897.
ÉMILE LEGOUIS, *William Wordsworth and Annette Vallon*. London and Toronto, 1922.
ÉMILE LEGOUIS, *Wordsworth in a New Light*, Cambridge, London, 1923.
SALVADOR DE MADARIAGA, *The Case of Wordsworth*. 1921.
LAURIE MAGNUS, *A Primer of Wordsworth with a critical Essay*. London, 1897.
F. W. H. MYERS, *Wordsworth*. London, 1880.
WALTER PATER, *Appreciations*. London, 1889.
P. H. PUGHE, *Studien über Byron und Wordsworth*. Heidelberg, 1902.
THOMAS DE QUINCEY, *Recollections of the Lakes and the Lake-poèts*. Edinburgh, 1862.
WALTER RALEIGH, *Wordsworth*. London, 1903.
MYRA REYNOLDS, *The Treatment of Nature in English Poetry between Pope and Wordsworth*. Chicago, 1897.
E. HERSHEY SNEATH, *Wordsworth, Poet of Nature and Poet of Man*. Boston and London, 1912.
ALGERNON CHARLES SWINBURNE, *Miscellanies*. A new Impression, London, 1911.
WILLIAMS WATSON, *Wordsworth's Grave*, 1884—87.
WILLIAMS WORDSWORTH and S. T. COLERIDGE. *Lyrical Ballads with an Advertisement*, London, 1798, edited with certain Poems of 1798 and an *Introduction and Notes* by Thomas Hutchinson. London, 1898.

BARRY CERF, *Wordsworth's Gospel of Nature*, Publications of the Modern Language Association, 1922.
The Critical Review VIII, 1793.
FRANCIS JEFFREY, *The Excursion*, Edinburgh Review, Nov. 1814. *The White Doe of Rylstone*, Ibid., Oct. 1815.
OSCAR CAMPBELL, *Wordsworth bandies Jests with Matthew*, Modern Language Notes, Nov. 1921.
A. CLUTTON—BROCK, *The Problem of Wordsworth*, The London Mercury, Oct. 1920.
ÉMILE LEGOUIS, *Reply to Edith Morley*, The literary Supplement of the Times, 8 March 1923.
ÉMILE LEGOUIS, *Dix ans de critique wordsworthienne*, Revue Anglo-Américaine VI, Aout 1926.
THE REV. J. P. LILLEY, *Wordsworth's Interpretation of Nature*, The Hibbert Journal XIX, 1920.
L. R. MERRILL, *Vaughan's Influence upon Wordsworth's Poetry*, Modern Language Notes I, Febr. 1922.
EDITH J. MORLEY, *Wordsworth's French Daughter*, The literary Supplement of the Times, 15 Febr. 1923.
HENRY S. PANCOAST, *Did Wordsworth jest with Matthews?* Modern Language Notes XXXVII, 1922.
GEORGE H. PALMER, *Review of Harper*, Harvard Theological Review, 1917.
W. P. RAWNSLEY, *New Light on Wordsworth*, Poetry Review VII, 1916. Review of Harper.
LESLIE WEATHERHEAD, *The Idea of Immortality in Wordsworth*, Quarterly Review, July, Oct. 1924.

STELLINGEN

I

Matthew Arnold's bewering: *"The Excursion* and *The Prelude* are by no means Wordsworth's best work," is met betrekking tot het laatste gedicht niet juist. (*Essays in Criticism*, p. 135. London, Macmillan and Co.)

II

Evelyn Underhill onderschat Wordsworth als mysticus, wanneer ze hem niet onder degenen rangschikt, voor wie "the veil is obliterated by the light behind," en "faith has vanished into sight." (*Mysticism*, p. 282. London, Methuen and Co.)

III

Barry Cerf's oordeel: "The real Wordsworth seems to have been the later," is niet juist. (*Publications of the Modern Language Association*, 1922.)

IV

Harper's bewering, dat Wordsworth in de *Prelude* het geloof verloochende, dat hij uitsprak in *Tintern Abbey*, is aanvechtbaar. (*William Wordsworth, his Life Work and Influence*, II, p. 148. London, John Murray.)

V

De verandering in punctuatie, die Garrod geeft in Wordsworth's *Prelude* I, 398—401,

"But huge and mighty forms, that do not live,
Like living men moved slowly through the mind
By day, and were a trouble to my dreams,

STELLINGEN

is onaannemelijk. (*Wordsworth: Lectures and Essays*, p. 33. Oxford, at the Clarendon Press.)

VI

Het is niet onwaarschijnlijk, dat de invloed van Coleridge op **Wordsworth** grooter was dan omgekeerd.

VII

Burdett's bewering: "Blake's manner is always convincing, his meaning not always," is onjuist. (*William Blake*, p. 189. London, Macmillan and Co.)

VIII

Hubbard's meening dat Defoe zijn onderwerp voor *Robinson Crusoe* uit Smeeks' *Krinke Kesmes* heeft genomen, is ongegrond. (*Sjouke Gabbes, a Dutch source for Robinson Crusoe*. Den Haag, 1921.)

IX

A. C. Bradley's bewering: "In Lady Macbeth there is no trace of contrition," is aanvechtbaar. (*Shakespearean Tragedy*, p. 378. London, Macmillan and Co.)

X

Onions' verandering van "sage" in "fage" in *Sir Gawayne and the Green Knight*, II, 530,
"and wynter wyndeʒ aʒain, as þe worlde askeʒ no sage,"
is niet noodig. (*The Literary Supplement of the Times*, 16 Aug. 1923.)

XI

In *Troilus and Cressida*, I, III, 237, is Theobald's lezing
"Good arms, strong joints, true swords; and, Jove's accord,
Nothing so full of heart,"
te verkiezen boven die van de oude drukken of de voorgestelde verbeteringen van Malone, Steevens en anderen.

XII

Voor het eindexamen H. B. S. is een staatsexamen te verkiezen boven een schoolexamen.